A Spacious Vision

A SPACIOUS VISION

Essays on Hardy

Edited by Phillip V. Mallett & Ronald P. Draper

The Patten Press
Newmill

First published in Great Britain in 1994
by the Patten Press (Publishers),
The Old Post Office, Newmill, Penzance, Cornwall TR20 4XN

ISBN 1 872229 12 3

Typesetting by Melissa Hardie at the Patten Press.
Cover design by Philip Budden
Designed and originated in-house

Printed and bound by the Cromwell Press,
Broughton Gifford, Melksham, Wiltshire

Contents

For Jim

DR. JAMES GIBSON

A Dedication

*T*owards the end of his Introduction to the Variorum Edition of the Poems of Thomas Hardy, which came at the climax of years of work on what is probably still the finest scholarly, and most appropriate, monument to Hardy's achievement as a poet, Jim Gibson writes: 'I am deeply aware that I have had the privilege of being associated with a writer who is truly great. My admiration for his creative genius, his integrity, the quality of his feeling, and the professionalism of his approach to his writing has grown with the years and made the labour eminently worthwhile.'

In the year of Jim's seventy-fifth birthday we cannot do better than echo those words which express Jim's own dedication throughout a remarkably productive career to promoting the enjoyment and understanding of all aspects of the writing of Thomas Hardy -- a career which has itself been stamped by integrity, quality of feeling and professionalism. Both as critic and editor Jim Gibson has made generations of readers more acutely aware of the sheer craftsmanship that goes into Hardy's novels, stories and poems. It is no longer possible to treat Hardy with the condescension of many critics in the past who regarded him as at once a naive artist and a ponderously inept 'autodidact'. Thanks to Jim's own work we have no excuse for being unaware of the patience and imaginative scrupulousness with which Hardy sought out the right word, the right phrase, the right order in his poetry, and it is very much owing to Jim's example and exhortation that similarly conscientious editors are now doing the same for Hardy's prose fiction. Whenever Hardy's work was reprinted it was subjected to careful revision, and such revision, as Jim shows in his 1980 essay on 'Hardy and his Readers' , was not just polishing and refining, but frequently a means by which Hardy put more of his true self into his work.

Jim, however, is far more than the Hardy textual scholar. The Macmillan Casebook, edited with Trevor Johnson, on *The Poems of Thomas Hardy,* and his earlier editions and selections of the poetry, including his audio-visual programme, *Thomas Hardy: The Making of Poetry*, testify to what seems to have been, and still is, his primary love among Hardy's work, i.e., the poetry. (This was the subject of his London University Ph.D. and is now the subject of his 1994 Hardy Conference lecture on 'Hardy's Poetry: Poetic Apprehension and Poetic Method'.) But his skill and energy in making Hardy's work available to students and the common reader as well as the Hardy specialist is also evident in the work he has done on the short stories and many of the novels, including *Far from the Madding Crowd, A Pair of Blue Eyes, Two on a Tower, Tess of the d'Urbervilles, The Woodlanders, Jude the Obscure* and *The Well-Beloved*. In 1975 he was appointed General Editor of the Macmillan Students' Hardy series, and his spreading of the Hardy good news has continued in countless lectures, radio talks, interviews and TV appearances, not only in Britain, but also in Austria, Holland and the U.S.A. Above all, as far as members of the Thomas Hardy Society are concerned, he is the Chairman of the Society who has committed his seemingly inexhaustible energy and ingenuity to organising, inspiring and serving as the indispensable adviser in all its meetings, conferences and Hardy promotional activities. And from 1985-1990 he was also the astonishingly creative Editor of the Society's *Journal*, which, largely owing to his efforts and expertise, became, and remains, the internationally recognised periodical devoted to Hardy studies.

That is still by no means all of Jim. He has had not one, but several distinguished careers, including those of schoolteacher and college lecturer. From 1949-1962 he was Head of the English Department at Dulwich College, a job which he loved. He obviously found teaching intelligent and enthusiastic sixth-formers expecially rewarding. In her book on Dulwich College Sheila Hodges comments on the good fortune the school had in attracting a group of exceptionally gifted young teachers in the period after the Second World War, but feels compelled to give special mention to Jim Gibson. One colleague described him as 'a missionary head of English'. He was clearly an inspirational teacher: the impression made on one of his pupils by a moving lesson on D.H. Lawrence's poem 'Piano' was so deep that he still retained vivid memories of it more than forty years after. Under his guidance the number of English 'O' and 'A' levels shot up and a string of pupils won scholarships to university. Jim himself was honoured by receiving the first invitation to take up a Schoolmaster Fellowship at Corpus Christi College, Cambridge.

In 1962 he went to Christ Church College, Canterbury as Principal Lecturer, and in due course became Head of the English Field. A succession of important chairmanships in the world of education administration followed, including the University of London's Board of Education Subject Committee in English, the Institute of Education Standing Committee in English, and the Board of Education Joint Subject Committee in English. He was also English examiner at 'O' and 'A' levels and for the University of London B.Ed. degree and the University of Kent B.A. [Christ Church] course. In addition, he published numerous books, including school text-books, anthologies and volumes in the Macmillan Masterworks series, of which he became General Editor in 1979.

Here, you might say, is God's plenty! Enough to constitute the life's work of half-a-dozen more ordinarily energetic and productive men; after which, you might think, he would be content to rest on his laurels. Indeed, such an address as his present one, in Abbot's Walk, Cerne Abbas, conjures up an image of venerable retirement and suggests the well-earned exchange of the *vita activa* for the *vita contemplativa*. But not so. Jim continues to be what he has always been -- a veritable ball of fire, drumming up support for the Hardy Society, publicising its activities as widely as possible, and fighting the cause of Hardy and his writings as doughtily as ever. A better champion, and a better cause, no one could ask for. Hardy is a great thing, a great thing to him. And the highest -- as well as, we would guess, the most welcome -- tribute we can pay Jim Gibson is our grateful acknowledgement of the way he keeps that greatness still so fresh in our minds.

PVM and RPD

Publisher's Note: Several of the essays contributed to this volume have been presented in different forms, as lectures, but none has been previously published. Acknowledgement is made to *The London Review of Books* for permission to reprint 'Colleague' and to *The Spectator* for the reprint of 'Evergreen' and 'John Sell Cotman at Rokeby', poems by Simon Curtis. The cover design by Philip Budden, on the softbound edition, incorporates a wood-engraving executed by Vivien Gribble for the 1926 (large-paper, 325 copies, signed by Thomas Hardy) Macmillan edition of *Tess of the d'Urbervilles*. The publisher and editors gratefully acknowledge grants in support of *A Spacious Vision: Essays on Hardy* from Christ Church College, Canterbury, the University of Aberdeen and the University of St Andrews.

A Cento of First Lines for James Gibson

I went by star and planet shine,
I went by the Druid stone.
The flame crept up the portrait line by line
Late on Christmas Eve, in the street alone,
Looking forward to the spring.

And the Spirit said
At midnight, in the room where he lay dead,
"Sing; how 'a would sing!
Sweet cyder is a great thing...
O that mastering tune!" And up in the bed

Phantasmal fears
Backward among the dusky years.
On the flat road a man at last appears:
Do you think of me at all,
Do you recall

Five lone clangs from the house-clock nigh,
Pale beech and pine so blue?
"It is a foolish thing", said I,
"Not a line of her writing have I.
There is not much that I can do."

ANTHONY THWAITE

See Index of First Lines, *The Complete Poems of Thomas Hardy*, edited by James Gibson, 1976: pages 96, 483, 405, 558, 273, 481, 391, 205, 414, 246, 507, 805, 702, 907, 792, 750, 40, 272, 38, 563.

Insects in Hardy's Fiction

Michael Irwin

Animals and birds play a significant part in Hardy's work, often involving not only the feelings but the fortunes of his characters. Henchard's love for Elizabeth-Jane is expressed by his gift of a caged goldfinch. The Durbeyfield family is ruined by the death of their horse. Gabriel Oak has his life saved by one dog and his livelihood destroyed by another. By contrast the fictional potentiality of insects would seem to be meagre. They do not engage our affections and save for the odd bite or sting are involved in few transactions with humankind. More than that: they are small, elusive, unnoticeable -- altogether out of scale with Man. How is a writer famous for his sharply-focused portrayal of character to achieve the descriptive depths of field to record anything beyond the peripheral presence of the occasional bee or butterfly? None the less insects are copiously represented in Hardy. There is no novel by him in which an insect doesn't make a creep-on, or fly-in, appearance. In many there is repeated reference to a separate, simultaneous world of tiny creatures: flies, crane-flies, bees, wasps, moths, butterflies, ants, beetles, grasshoppers, gnats, woodlice, caterpillars, snails and slugs. No doubt Hardy acquires an extra edge of authority from the implied acuity of apprehension. 'He was a man who used to notice such things': since he is sensitive to sights and sounds so small we are the more likely to trust his observation elsewhere. But it would take more than this to justify the presence of so many insects. Why and how does Hardy introduce them? In what ways, if any, do their miniaturised activities display the workings of his imagination?

At first glance these frequent references might seem to represent no more than an extension of his general respect and consideration for all living creatures. In 'An August Midnight', when the longlegs, the moth, the dumbledore and the fly invade Hardy's desk and 'besmear my new-penned line', he shows no impatience. 'Thus meet we five', he observes, democratically. This sympathy is widely observable in the novels. In the last of them the young Jude treads carefully lest he crush an earthworm (*JO*, 11). In one of the first Geoffrey Day shows himself anxious to treat his bees with humanity: '"The proper way to take honey, so that the bees be neither starved nor murdered is a puzzling matter."' He avoids the new method of fumigation because it means that '"the pangs o'

1

death be twice upon 'em'". Even when repeatedly stung by some bees trapped in his clothing he comments with placid sympathy: "'...they can't sting me many times more, poor things; for they must be getting weak'" (*UGT*, 146-7). By contrast it's probably an ominous sign that Sergeant Troy, in the sword-play scene, casually executes a caterpillar to show off his fencing skills.

'An August Midnight' also implies that there might be something to be learnt from insects: 'They know Earth-secrets that know not I'. Hardy's 'native' characters can interpret nature's signs: there may be hidden significance in the conduct of cattle or birds. The truly adept pick up still slighter signals. Gabriel Oak recognises omens of an impending storm in the doings of a toad, a slug and two spiders before seeking confirmation in the reactions of his sheep. Insects provide meteorological and ecological small print for those equipped to read it.

But Hardy frequently invokes them for subtler, more 'philosophical' purposes. In *Desperate Remedies*, his first novel, the idiosyncrasy is already evident. A notable example is the scene which follows Manston's proposal to Cytherea and her rejection of him. Left to himself he stares into a water-butt:

> The reflection from the smooth stagnant surface tinged his face with the greenish shades of Correggio's nudes. Staves of sunlight slanted down through the still pool, lighting it up with wonderful distinctness. Hundreds of thousands of minute living creatures sported and tumbled in its depth with every contortion that gaiety could suggest; perfectly happy, though consisting only of a head, or a tail, or at most a head and a tail, and all doomed to die within the twenty-four hours.

Technically these roisterers aren't insects, but they're close enough for the purposes of this essay. On casual reading the passage seems incidental, a descriptive interlude in a densely plotted 'sensation novel'. Further thought suggests that a good deal more is going on. There can be little doubt that Hardy wants us to respond attentively: the scene is sharply lit and carefully composed -- as the reference to Correggio hints. We are shown not only the 'minute living creatures' but Manston himself contemplating them, reacting to them. The sight influences his thinking, determining him to persist in his advances: "'Why shouldn't I be happy through my little day too?'" But it isn't that the episode has been imposed on the text to bring about a change of mood required by the plot. At this stage in the novel the action has faded into indistinctness; somehow Cytherea is to be unwillingly drawn towards marriage with Manston. There's no serious chance that he'll give up the chase. It seems likely that the proposal scene, perfunctorily disposed of in two sentences, has itself been thrown in as an excuse for the introduction of the water-butt and its thought-provoking contents. For Hardy the interpolation has intrinsic weight. It gains greater importance retrospectively, when we find that Manston's reactions, far from being whimsical, are all of a piece with his farewell letter, which emphasises the brevity of life:

I am now about to enter on my normal condition. For people are almost always in their graves. When we survey the long race of men, it is strange and still more strange to find that they are mainly dead men, who have scarcely ever been otherwise.

It is the very insignificance of the tiny swimmers that prompts Manston to speculation and shapes his mood. Shortly afterwards Cytherea herself is similarly influenced:

On the right hand the sun, resting on the horizon-line, streamed across the ground from below copper-coloured clouds, stretched out in flats beneath a sky of pale soft green. All dark objects on the earth that lay towards the sun were overspread by a purple haze, against which a swarm of wailing gnats shone forth luminously, rising upward and floating away like sparks of fire.

The stillness oppressed and reduced her to mere passivity. The only wish the humidity of the place left in her was to stand motionless. The helpless flatness of the landscape gave her, as it gives all such temperaments, a sense of bare equality with, and no superiority to, a single entity under the sky.

Here, of course, the scene is fuller, and the part played by the insects is less central. Neither character nor author interprets. Only implicitly is it suggested that the evening light, the humidity, the flatness make Cytherea feel of no more account than a gnat. But as with the water-butt episode the very motives of the watcher are influenced: Cytherea senses that she is drifting listlessly towards marriage. Again the incident is unnecessary to the plot: nothing comes of it directly or immediately. Yet in both cases Hardy is writing with passion and scrupulosity. The prose is intent, evocative, rhythmical. Light and colour are powerfully observed, in this second case serving to transfigure and beautify the 'swarm of wailing gnats'.

It is a measure of Hardy's involvement in these two passages that both are re-worked in *The Return of the Native*. Several sentences from the sunset-scene are repeated verbatim (208-9), here providing the context in which Clym is persuaded to fix a marriage-date with Eustacia. Again there is an echo of Keats's 'Ode to Autumn' as 'wailing gnats' dance luminously in the light of the sunset, but this time both lovers feel oppressed. The mood of the occasion, 'this overpowering of the fervid by the inanimate', is sufficiently marked and distinctive for Hardy to recall it a hundred pages later (328), when Clym returns from Susan Nunsuch's cottage to make his accusations against Eustacia.

On her ill-fated visit to her married son Mrs. Yeobright pauses from time to time to watch, like Manston, 'ephemerons ... in mad carousal':

> ...some in the air, some on the hot ground and vegetation, some in the tepid and stringy water of a nearly dried pool. All the shallower ponds had decreased to a vaporous mud, amid which the maggoty shapes of innumerable obscene creatures could be indistinctly seen, heaving and wallowing with enjoyment. Being a woman not disinclined to philosophise she sometimes sat down under her umbrella to rest and to watch their happiness...(278)

This vignette is more complex in its effect than its predecessor in *Desperate Remedies*. The tone is equivocal. 'Enjoyment', 'happiness', even 'mad carousal' are positive terms; 'maggoty', 'obscene', 'heaving and wallowing' pull the other way. Since Mrs. Yeobright is preoccupied with thoughts of Clym it's hardly fanciful to see this ambiguity as reflecting mixed impulses: hope concerning the outcome of her visit compounded with distaste for her son's relationship with 'a voluptuous idle woman'. What she sees both images and intensifies what she feels.

The passage proves to be part of a sequence -- extending over several chapters, and culminating in Mrs. Yeobright's death -- in which the sights and sounds of Egdon Heath are made to provide a commentary on the doings of the Yeobrights and, by extension, of human-beings in general. Plants, trees and birds are all featured, but insects predominate. Mrs. Yeobright follows a furzecutter who appears 'of a russet hue, not more distinguishable from the scene around him than the green caterpillar from the leaf it feeds on'. He seems 'of no more account than an insect' -- 'a mere parasite of the heath'. Only belatedly does she realise that the man she has been seeing as thus belittled is Clym himself. In Clym's own garden she notices wasps 'rolling drunk' with the juice of the apples they have been eating, 'stupefied by its sweetness'. To her mind, of course, Clym has been similarly 'stupefied' by the charms of Eustacia.

Later, returning homeward, sad and weary after what she takes to be a rebuff, she sits and watches a colony of ants, 'a never-ending and heavy-laden throng': 'To look down upon them was like observing a city street from the top of a tower'. A comment from Johnny Nunsuch, a page or two earlier, has provided a hint, if a hint is needed, as to the significance of such allusions:

> Once when I went to Throope Great Pond to catch effets I seed myself looking up at myself, and I was frightened and jumped back like anything. (288)

What Hardy's characters see in the doings of insects, as in nature at large, is a reflection of their own condition.

Of all the novels *The Return of the Native* is the one in which the author makes the most frequent and the most calculated references to insects. The instances quoted above can be placed within a much fuller metaphorical context, a Modernist exercise in patterning, involving all four main characters. Even prior to Mrs. Yeobright's journey Clym has been shown at work among 'creeping and winged things' (253-4) that 'seemed to enrol him in their band'. He moves among bees, 'amber-coloured butterflies' and 'emerald-green grasshoppers'. Earlier still Eustacia, 'in her winter dress' has been likened to 'the tiger-beetle which, when observed in dull situations, seems to be of the quietest neutral colour, but under a full illumination blazes with dazzling splendour' (88).

Every reader of the novel will recall the bizarre scene where Wildeve and Diggory Venn gamble by the light of glow-worms. They are reduced to this pass because 'a large death's-head moth' has flown into their lantern and extinguished it. That accident finds a later echo when Wildeve invites Eustacia to an assignation by means of a moth. He slips it into the partly open window and it blunders into the candle flame. She immediately recognises the signal that he had used for the same purpose in the old days at Mistover.

Later, when Clym returns to Blooms-End, after his mother's death, he finds that 'a spider had already constructed a large web tying the door to the lintel, on the supposition that it was never to be opened again' (321). The abandoned house intensifies his sense of desolation. '"My life creeps like a snail"', he tells Diggory Venn. Everywhere the characters go they are somehow involved with 'an unseen insect world'.

It has become a critical commonplace to see Hardy's descriptions of nature, in general, not as mere 'background', but as figurative context. The simplest recurring metaphorical inference is that Man, in his littleness and helplessness, is akin to an animal, a bird, a tree -- or an insect. It is surely in this vein that Hardy describes Tess and Marian at work in the swede-field as 'crawling ... like flies' (277), or compares a busy highway to 'an ant-walk' *(T-M)* or sees soldiers at work as 'busying themselves like cheese-mites' (*Dynasts* 290). Insects are so small, so ubiquitously numerous, that their teeming presence is a continual reminder that each of us is 'one of a long row only'. The astronomer Swithin St. Cleeve feels himself 'annihilated' by his nightly study of 'monsters of magnitude' (*TT* 33). The violent shifts of perspective to which he subjects himself are, of course, only an extremer version of those experienced by many a character in the fiction of Hardy, whose heroes and heroines regularly wield telescopes. It would come as no great surprise to hear of a lost Hardy novel which featured a scientist demoralised by regular use of a microscope to investigate 'monsters of minitude' -- indeed Fitzpiers is such a character in embryo. Equally with the dizzyingly large the dizzyingly small can dramatise an impartial relativity in the universe, wholly unflattering to Man's pretensions.

In *The Life* Hardy offers an interesting variation on this idea, in terms of a piquant inversion. He is quoting a journal entry:

'28 Nov. I sit under a tree, and feel alone: I think of certain insects around me as magnified by the microscope: creatures like elephants, flying dragons, etc. And I feel I am by no means alone.' (*Life*, 110)

Again the sense is equivocal. If 'lonely' were substituted, in both sentences, for 'alone', the emphasis would be curiously companionable. 'Curiously' in that most of us would prefer a spell of loneliness to an encounter with an elephant-sized bug. The point isn't a frivolous one. Hardy seems to share the ambiguous attitude to insect-life displayed by many of his characters. On the one hand the friendly anthropomorphism of 'An August Midnight', where the 'sleepy fly that rubs its hands' is greeted as 'my guest'; on the other the blighting comparisons that reduce a human being to the level of an ant or a cheese-mite.

Perhaps relevant to this ambiguity is the recurrent emphasis, in relevant descriptions, on two apparently unrelated factors. One, already mentioned in passing, is the vividness of feeling attributed to the insects or associated with them. The ephemerons are 'heaving and wallowing with enjoyment', a wasp may be 'rolling drunk' or 'tipsy' (*Woodlanders*, 233), the gnats 'wailing' or 'dancing up and down in airy companies' (*T-M* 182). Cows, in *Tess* (151) jump 'wildly over the five-barred barton-gate, maddened by the gad-fly'. Mrs. Charmond complains bitterly (*Woodlanders* 252): '"I lay awake last night, and I could hear the scrape of snails creeping up the window glass; it was so sad!"' Even in these smallest of nature's manifestations there is an intensity of life which serves to enlarge one's sense of the far greater intensity within the human protagonists.

The other repeated emphasis, already illustrated in the two passages from *Desperate Remedies*, is on vivid lighting effects: 'singing insects hung in every sunbeam' (*Woodlanders* 263). Because Marty South's house is in 'an exceptional state of radiance', Percomb is able to see 'every now and then a moth, decrepit from the late season' (45-6). The night before he is posted away from Overcombe John Loveday sits in darkness by the mill-pond and peers up at Anne Garland's bedroom: 'The light shone out upon the broad and deep mill-head, illuminating to a distinct individuality every moth and gnat that entered the quivering chain of radiance...' Anne herself looks out at the scene 'for some time', but never guesses that John is there. During the period when Tess is prevaricating over the date of her wedding she often idles out of doors with Angel Clare:

Looking over the damp sod in the direction of the sun a glistening ripple of gossamer-webs was visible to their eyes under the luminary, like the track of moonlight on the sea. Gnats, knowing nothing of their brief glorification, wandered across the shimmer of this pathway, irradiated as if they bore fire within them; then passed out of its line, and were quite extinct. In the presence of these things he would remind her that the date was still the question. (200)

The description and the situation are reminiscent of both *Desperate Remedies* and *The Return of the Native*. Here, too, the implied metaphor is a comment on the brevity of human happiness and human life. The word 'irradiated' deserves some attention. In the otherwise subdued coda to *The Mayor of Casterbridge* the life of Elizabeth-Jane, now happily married to Farfrae, is described as 'suddenly irradiated'. After Tess has 'confessed' to Angel Clare they go for a miserable nightwalk. She notices the stars reflected in the small puddles of water created by the footprints of cattle: 'the vastest things of the universe imaged in objects so mean.' Clare, she knows, sees her 'without irradiation -- in all her bareness'. She has enjoyed no more than a 'brief glorification', like that of the gnats. The echoed word confirms that the 'radiance' recurrent in these descriptions is suggestive of a momentary joy and beauty. More mundanely, of course, the bright light may be necessary to enable the tiny insects to be seen at all -- but it also dramatises the significance in their doings. It illuminates in more senses than one -- and the observer may or may not like what is seen.

A *Pair of Blue Eyes* includes an episode that offers a diagram of the process. Shortly after Stephen Smith's return from India, and while he is still miserably uncertain concerning the state of Elfride's affections, he goes walking at night and hears her voice. He watches as she and the man she is with enter a summer-house:

The scratch of a striking light was heard, and a glow radiated from the interior of the building. The light gave birth to dancing leaf-shadows, lustrous streaks, dots, sparkles, and threads of silver sheen of all imaginable variety and transience. It awakened gnats, which flew towards it, revealed shiny gossamer threads, disturbed earthworms. Stephen gave but little attention to these phenomena, and less time. He saw in the summer-house a strongly illuminated picture. (236)

As often in Hardy the light in the darkness is both literal and metaphorical. Here the insects are incidental, their reactions a by-product of the 'illumination' that Elfride has transferred her affections to Smith's best friend. In several of the passages quoted earlier an unusual intensity of light serves solely to display or 'glorify' the insects, which provide a purely metaphorical revelation. As he gazes into the water-butt Manston sees 'with wonderful distinctness' not merely the ephemerons but a certain aspect of life. In Hardy terms he experiences a 'moment of vision'.

Hardy's habit of metaphor is densely associative. Repeatedly his imagery suggests that any given aspect of nature partakes of others. In *Tess*, for example, cows are described as having teats 'as hard as carrots'; there is 'a monstrous pumpkin-like moon'; the heroine herself is likened to a bird, a cat, a sapling, a flower -- as well as a fly. Insects regularly feature in such comparisons. Birch-trees are said to 'put on their new leaves, delicate as butterflies' wings' (*RN* 589), cow-slips seem to give out a light 'as from...glow-worms' (*Life* 112), children in school are heard 'humming small, like a swarm of gnats' (*JO* 211). Frequently such images, or implied images, seem to involve not mere similitude, but assimilation. The entities compared reveal virtually a common charac-teristic, or engage in virtually a common activity. In *Two on a Tower* (173) Hardy describes a Sunday-morning scene amid a blaze of spring flowers:

The animate things that moved amid this scene of colour were plodding bees, gadding butterflies, and numerous sauntering young feminine candi-dates for the impending confirmation, who, having gaily bedecked them-selves for the ceremony, were enjoying their own appearance by walking about in twos and threes till it was time to start.

The girls here seem not essentially distinguishable from the 'gadding butterflies': both species wander in the sunshine, delighting in self-display.

In *The Woodlanders*, when Fitzpiers has just made his first clear advances to Grace Melbury, there is a sudden diversion: 'two large birds...apparently en-grossed in a desperate quarrel' tumble into the hot ashes of an open-air fire and singe their wings. '"That's the end of what is called love,"' observes Marty South, who happens to be passing and has not seen Grace or Fitzpiers. Hardy is well below his best here. The symbol would seem extrinsic and contrived even without Marty's implausible interpretative apostrophe. Birds don't charac-teristically fly into fires; they are made to do so here solely for the sake of a metaphor. The effect apparently intended is more elegantly achieved by the poem 'The Moth-Signal' and the parallel episode in *The Return of the Native*. In both cases Hardy is at pains to stress that the moth lured to the candle is 'burnt and broken', as will be the lover drawn by the flame of passion. But here the symbolism doesn't seem forced, because the two processes described are equally instinctual and perhaps equally likely to prove destructive.

When Anne Loveday watches the *Victory* depart (*T-M* 293) she sees it diminish until 'no more than a dead fly's wing on a sheet of spider's web'. Conversely *The Hand of Ethelberta* (244-5) features a seaside prospect in which 'a white butterfly among the apple-trees might be mistaken for the sails of a yacht far away on the sea'. The complementary images represent a more orthodox version of the shift of perspective seen in the passage from the *Life*, and they make more than a visual point. The things compared are in effect the same thing: the butterfly's wings function as sails; the sails of the ship are man-made wings.

There's a Darwinian implication here. Man and insect are fellow species, driven by similar impulses, struggling to survive with the capacities at their command, some of which they have in common. In our different ways, and perhaps for different ends, we shrink from the rain, bask in the sun, ride on the wind. We can have conflicts of interest, often mortal to the insects. In *The Woodlanders* Fitzpiers watches as three girls, Suke Damson, Marty South and Grace Melbury, cope, or fail to cope with the challenge of a newly-painted gate (161-2). The first two soil their clothes; the more alert Grace pushes the sticky gate aside with a twig, and passes unscathed. More hapless victims are the gnats which 'stuck dying thereon'. It could be argued that the gnats and the human passers-by are fellow-sufferers. On the other hand the problem in this case is one that men alone could cause, and men alone could solve -- as Grace does. Deliberately or involuntarily human-beings can wreak havoc in the insect world. As Tess and her friends walk to Mellstock Church 'Their gauzy skirts had brushed up from the grass innumerable flies and butterflies which, unable to escape, remained caged in the transparent tissue as in an aviary' (146). Paula Power stands by the fire (*Laodicean* 208) and notices 'the wood-lice which ran approached them'. The mill in *The Trumpet-Major* is the home of Loveday, the Garlands -- and also a variety of insects and other small creatures. Some of these fall victim to the human inhabitants. The Miller and his son Bob talk of the ubiquitous brown and black slugs, and 'of the relative exterminatory merits of a pair of scissors and the heel of the shoe'. The great clean-up which precedes Matilda's arrival inflicts carnage: 'The upper floors were scrubbed with such abundance of water that the old-established death-watches, wood-lice and flour-worms were all drowned...' (131).

The insects, however, make encroachments on their own account. In Bath-sheba Everdene's house the floorboards have been 'eaten into innumerable vermiculations'. The very cupboards Mrs. Garland is cleaning are 'worm-eaten' -- as, eventually, will be the pikes of the local militia (196 and Preface). Man and insect are locked powerlessly into a scheme of mutual depredation. The oak coffer where Miller Loveday has kept his wardrobe encloses a 'hard stratification of old jackets, waistcoats, and knee-breeches at the bottom, never disturbed since the miller's wife died, and half pulverised by the moths, whose flattened skeletons lay amid the mass in thousands'. The moths have destroyed the clothes; the clothes have crushed the moths: there remains a powdery precipitate of lifeless matter.

In a passage from *The Return of the Native* already referred to, Clym Yeobright, furzecutting on the heath, is said to be 'fretting its surface in his daily labour as a moth frets the garment'. Again the encroachments are reciprocal: later the heath will in its own way devour his wife and his mother. The biblical phrase recurs near the end of *The Well-Beloved* (in both versions), when Marcia has shown Pierston her now elderly face devoid of make-up: '"I am sorry if I shock you... But the moth frets the garment somewhat in such an interval."' As in the Old Testament, the image is of the stealthy erosion of beauty by natural processes. The preceding paragraph has proposed a harsher series of metaphors: 'To this the face he once kissed had been brought by the raspings, chisellings, scourgings, bakings, freezings of forty invidious years...' (200). Raspings and chisellings are resonant words in a novel centrally concerned with sculpture. Stone itself is not immune to such 'fretting'. We have seen how the very rock on which the main characters dwell has been cut up by saws to provide the raw materials for statues and buildings. Everywhere there is erosion and dissolution.

Stone of different kinds features regularly in Hardy's novels, often to image an enduring strength that must none-the-less yield to time. Insects are insignificant, ephemeral, frail to near-invisibility, the very slightest emanation of life -- yet can be touched with joy or glory in their brief existences. The fossilised trilobite in A Pair of Blue Eyes has survived for millions of years, but without such 'irradiation'. In their different ways, on their different time-scales, rock and insect represent the processes of change and evolution in which the human players are as inevitably trapped. Because that very process is intrinsic to Hardy's 'series of seemings', the ant, the fly and the caterpillar are far from incidental to his purposes.

NOTE

References given parenthetically in the text are to the World's Classics edition of the novels, and to The Life and Work of Thomas Hardy, edited by Michael Millgate (London, 1984) cited as Life.

Hardy's Style of the Moment

Dale Kramer

For decades, Hardy was criticized and scorned for the awkwardness of his prose and structure, perhaps most strongly in the 1950s and 1960s; then textual research from the 1960s to the 1980s turned up more than enough evidence that Hardy gave close attention to his novels. Both of these patterns of emphasis in Hardy criticism are well enough known that I omit documenting them. What I want to concentrate on, as a way of honouring James Gibson's vigorous attention to precise details and images in Hardy's poetry, are some ways in which Hardy makes good use of small touches in one of his stories, *The Mayor of Casterbridge*.

In choosing this novel to provide focus for my remarks, obviously I am conscious that it is in relation to *The Mayor of Casterbridge* that Hardy expressed his best-known reservation about his skills as a novelist, saying (in the third-person voice of his autobiography) that *The Mayor of Casterbridge* 'was a story which Hardy fancied he had damaged more recklessly as an artistic whole, in the interest of the newspaper in which it appeared serially, than perhaps any other of his novels, his aiming to get an incident into almost every week's part causing him in his own judgment to add events to the narrative somewhat too freely. However as at this time he called his novel-writing "mere journeywork", he cared little about it as art, though it must be said in favour of the plot, as he admitted later, that it was quite coherent and organic, in spite of its complication [by which he seems to have meant complexity and crowdedness].' [1]

In fact, this observation as recorded by Hardy is anachronistic and misdirected. It was made in relation to the serial version of *The Mayor*: by the time of the book version, many of these sensational events had been removed, including a fuller description of the pursuit of Elizabeth-Jane and Lucetta by the bull, and a nocturnal meeting of Henchard and Lucetta in the Amphitheatre interrupted by Farfrae (who doesn't recognize his wife in disguise). Thus the book version of the novel is not as seriously marred in the way Hardy recollected his original strategy in composing the novel. Also, Hardy was thinking of large structural or plot events, while small touches in the novel more modestly but not the less influentially associated with 'style' have a much more positive bearing. This bearing is crucial in providing readers with clues about how to read the novel. I classify Hardy's style as 'of the present' because its most pronounced impact occurs during the immediate act of reading. It has long-term resonance also, but what dominates are the moments of transient liveliness and the persuasiveness of plausible, unexcited insights into the nature of communication.

In the years preceding *The Mayor of Casterbridge* Hardy was thinking about the principles of art and of fiction in particular, and he recorded his preference for uncommonness and improbabilities in incident rather than in character (*Life and Work*, p. 183) and his view that 'so-called simplicity' may be 'simplicity of the highest cunning' (*Life and Work*, p. 177). Thus, the supposed indifferent artistry of *The Mayor of Casterbridge* can be expected to reflect a more individualistic or at least more considered aesthetic than the earlier novels. And certainly it is true that in the novels after *The Mayor of Casterbridge* -- *The Woodlanders, Tess of the d'Urbervilles, The Well-Beloved*, and *Jude the Obscure* -- Hardy further experimented with form and meaning and societal orientation in vital and forceful ways.

The aspects of Hardy's style I want to comment on are interrelated. For example, the mythic quality of language in this novel can scarcely be separated from the simple directness of Hardy's manner, which in serious contexts carries within it a suggestion of the ritual necessity at the heart of folk beliefs. As an instance, consider how Henchard's formulaic behaviour after the wife-sale defines the narrator's reference to 'something fetichistic in this man's beliefs':

He shouldered his basket and moved on, casting his eyes inquisitively round upon the landscape as he walked, and at the distance of three or four miles perceived the roofs of a village and the tower of a church. He instantly made towards the latter object. The village was quite still, it being that motionless hour of rustic daily life which fills the interval between the departure of the field-labourers to their work, and the rising of their wives and daughters to prepare the breakfast for their return. Hence he reached the church without observation, and the door being only latched he entered. The hay-trusser deposited his basket by the font, went up the nave till he reached the altar-rails, and opening the gate entered the sacrarium, where he seemed to feel a sense of the strangeness for a moment; then he knelt upon the foot-pace. Dropping his head upon the clamped book which lay on the Communion-table, he said aloud:

'I, Michael Henchard, on this morning of the sixteenth of September, do take an oath before God here in this solemn place that I will avoid all strong liquors for the space of twenty-one years to come, being a year for every year that I have lived. And this I swear upon the Book before me; and may I be strook dumb, blind, and helpless, if I break this my oath.'

When he had said it and kissed the big book, the hay-trusser arose, and seemed relieved at having made a start in a new direction. While standing in the porch a moment, he saw a thick jet of wood smoke suddenly start up from the red chimney of a cottage near, and knew that the occupant had just lit her fire. He went round to the door, and the housewife agreed to prepare him some breakfast for a trifling payment, which was done. Then he started on the search for his wife and child. [2]

The final sentence of this passage -- 'Then he started on the search for his wife and child' -- is at once climactic, predictive, and open-ended. Its simplicity is direct and homely, unpretentious as in all myth deeply rooted in customary behaviour. On a second reading of the novel, it is also wrenching and pitiable, for the reader aware of the novel's outcome knows that Henchard despite twenty years of expiation and acceptance of blame never finds his daughter: he only thinks he does, and after learning the truth of Elizabeth-Jane's identity he attempts (eventually, and unsuccessfully) to substitute the live Elizabeth-Jane for his daughter.

There is a long-standing debate among critics and readers of Hardy as to whether Henchard's fate is determined by his long-ago wife-sale -- whether this violation of basic human bonds is reflected in the moral sickness of Mixen Lane, in a way similar to the plague in Thebes being a consequence of Oedipus's murder of his father and marriage with his mother. There does not appear to be a resolution to this debate, but the style of the novel bolsters the mythic suggestiveness of the wife-sale, an underscoring made all the more effective by the contrasting force of such literal facts as the real bread that 'plims' folks' insides and the dance under tarpaulins stretched between trees. Similarly, the last sentence of the chapter containing Henchard's oath -- which with Chapter I forms the prolegomenon to the bulk of the novel -- in its suggestion of excessiveness builds a foundation for an action larger in its connotations than reality justifies: 'Next day he started, journeying south-westward, and did not pause, except for nights' lodgings, till he reached the town of Casterbridge, in a far distant part of Wessex' (p. 20). The implication that he takes himself to exile in Casterbridge is strikingly dramatic but factually a bit hyperbolic even before the completion of the railway system, in that Dorchester while 'far' from Bristol and farther from Liverpool (the two most likely debarkation points for Susan and Newson's rumoured emigration, and thus the place of Henchard's decision) is only 40 or so miles from one and some 80 miles from the other. Moreover, in contrast to the phrasing's suggestion of self-isolation from import-ant human doings, Dorchester is, and was, the county town, the centre for commerce in its area -- which is indeed precisely why Henchard during his initial, energetic phase succeeds there so handsomely.

The economy of language in these passages is characteristic of the spare, nearly-telegraphic prose that allows Hardy to achieve complex interactions of ideas and emotions within a compact passage. For another instance, one may consider the conversation between Lucetta and Elizabeth-Jane following Lu-cetta's remark that, in an earlier meeting of the three in the marketplace, 'Your father was distant with you':

'Yes'; and having forgotten the momentary mystery of Henchard's seeming
speech to Lucetta [Elizabeth-Jane had thought she heard Henchard murmur, "You refused to see me!"] she continued, "It is because he does not
. think I am respectable. I have tried to be so more than you can imagine,
but in vain! My mother's separation from my father was unfortunate for
me. You don't know what it is to have shadows like that upon your life."

Lucetta seemed to wince. 'I do not -- of that kind precisely,' she said; 'but
you may feel a -- sense of disgrace -- shame -- in other ways.'

'Have you ever had any such feeling?" said the younger innocently.' 'Oh
no,' said Lucetta quickly.'I was thinking of -- what happens sometimes
when women get themselves in strange positions in the eyes of the world
from no fault of their own.'

'It must make them very unhappy afterwards.'

'It makes them anxious; for might not other women despise them?'

'Not altogether despise them. Yet not quite like or respect them.'
    (pp. 170-71)

The loaded word in this passage is 'innocently', for the passage is conveying the
moment of Elizabeth-Jane's movement from blindness to knowledge concerning the complex of feelings among Lucetta, Henchard, and Farfrae. Elizabeth-
Jane evidently instantly understands that the reference in Lucetta's 'a -- sense
of disgrace -- shame' is sexual, for otherwise her statement that other women
might 'not quite like or respect' women with a shadow upon their lives would
be in reference to her own kind of 'shadow', but the way in which Henchard
thinks her not 'respectable' clearly is of a different order than her view of a
woman in the situation Lucetta posits. In other words, although avoiding an
explicit statement Hardy in this scene points up a permeative aspect to
Elizabeth-Jane's role vis-à-vis matters of deepest concern to her. Her perspective is brought closer to that of the narrator and, of equal significance in this
novel patterned on Greek tragedy, she is made to function in a way analogous
to that of the chorus, that is, to direct the reader's attention to a movement in
the 'argument' or 'plot'. Within two paragraphs of this passage, Elizabeth-Jane
with the prescience of a 'seer' or 'witch' has divined events 'so surely from data
already her own that they could be held as witnessed' (p. 171), so that she
imagines a meeting 'as if by chance' between Farfrae and Lucetta in such detail
that when Lucetta returns from a walk her countenance declares 'it was all true
as she [Elizabeth-Jane] had pictured' (p. 172). The choric function has acquired
a force capable of determining events, or at least accurately anticipating them,
a force whose credibility survives the simultaneous modification by the possibility that Elizabeth is biased ('she could have sworn it').

That an individual character has a choric dimension opens the relevance of
the narrator in a consideration of Hardy's style, the last aspect of the 'style of

14

the moment' in *The Mayor of Casterbridge* I want to review. If the narrator is thought to be that agent in fiction many readers turn to in sorting out those elements of a narrative on which they can rely, Hardy in this novel dissolves the conventional status of the narrator. In part this is owing to the overwhelmingly dominant role of Henchard in shaping the presentation of events. That is, not even the narrator has greater authority than the elemental, intellectually limited Henchard. Hardy's narratorial strategies assume that knowledge is based on perception, and perception by its nature is circumstantial and contingent, inherently 'of the moment'.

Uncertainty of knowledge -- even knowledge about the persons closest to us -- is exhibited in *The Mayor of Casterbridge* by the narrator. The narrator projects a combination of assertiveness and uncertainty, in a manner quite similar to the directive but vacillating intellect in the background of Greek drama, manipulative but often reduced by the time of the denouement to iterations of shattered values. The narrator of *The Mayor of Casterbridge* alternates between detachment and a rooted personalism. This offers perspectival freedom, illustrated in the novel's opening scene. The narrator moves from a great distance from the pedestrians Henchard and Susan (who is carrying the infant Elizabeth-Jane), offering several possible interpretations of their silence, up to a closer, cheek-by-jowl view during which the narrator not only 'reads' Susan's mobile face but also enters directly into her mind, all the while placing the couple's situation while they walk within an understanding of what has occurred on the hill 'for centuries untold' -- adding however 'the scene for that matter being one that might have been matched at almost any spot in any county in England at this time of the year' (pp. 5-6). This perspectival freedom is recurrent in the novel, as when during Henchard and Farfrae's fight the phrase 'as could be seen' in a reference to a twitching of pain on Henchard's face (p. 273) reminds the reader that although in one sense the two are alone, in another they continue the objects of a spectator's gaze. Although the freedom allows the narrator to speak of characters as acquaintances (p. 66 [the pupils of Elizabeth-Jane's eyes 'always seemed to have a red spark of light in them']) and to predict occasionally a plot development (p. 89 ['to which the future held the key']; p. 97 ['the seed that was to lift the foundation of this friendship was at that moment taking root in a chink of its structure']), the dominant tone of the narrator is detachment, with primarily external observation of Henchard and with only occasional examination of private feelings of others. The resulting overall impression is of suppressed personal or emotional involvement.

Another trait of the Greek chorus present in the characterization of the narrator of *The Mayor of Casterbridge* is the narrator's participation as a quality of drama, of situational tension of adventitiousness and inconsistency, in short. For instance -- perhaps to increase the mysteriousness attendant upon unexpected death -- the narrator with discreet sympathy notes, near the end of Lucetta's anguished suffering from the skimmington's mockery of her, 'What, and how much, Farfrae's wife ultimately explained to him of her past entanglement with Henchard, when they were alone in the solitude of that sad night, cannot be told' (p. 288); but when the narrator wishes to justify Farfrae's

15

decision not to pursue and prosecute the skimmington performers responsible for his wife's death, the point is made that 'Lucetta had confessed everything to him before her death, and it was not altogether desirable to make much ado about her history, alike for her sake, for Henchard's ,and for his own' (p. 300). Although the second passage is filtered through Farfrae, the material fact being conveyed -- Lucetta had 'confessed everything' -- is not diluted by a special perspective, and it is a flat contradiction of the denial of communication in the earlier passage. There is no implication that the narrator is flailing about uncertainly; rather, the narrator clearly is varying the terms of presentation in subtle ways so as to heighten a momentary effect. 'Truth' is in the instant of narration at least as much as in the always receding instant of occurrence. What is conveyed is neither ignorance nor deception, but immediacy and transience.

The enigmatic focus of the narrator increases the difficulty of judging the characters, and indeed makes judging by narrator or reader almost irrelevant. This applies, perhaps most strikingly, to the novel's summarizing moment of judgment, when the narrator displays Elizabeth-Jane as a fusion of universal and personal resolution of (to speak in general terms) the novel's position on meaning. The context of this resolution, however, seems to be the need to accommodate, within a social vision of continuity, Henchard's bleak and devastating personal vision:

Her experience had been of a kind to teach her, rightly or wrongly, that the doubtful honour of a brief transit through a sorry world hardly called for effusiveness, even when the path was suddenly irradiated at some half-way point by daybeams rich as hers. But her strong sense that neither she nor any human being deserved less than was given, did not blind her to the fact that there were others receiving less who had deserved much more. And in being forced to class herself among the fortunate she did not cease to wonder at the persistence of the unforeseen, when the one to whom such unbroken tranquillity had been accorded in the adult stage was she whose youth had seemed to teach that happiness was but the occasional episode in a general drama of pain. (pp. 334-35)

The quality of irony employed in this meditation permeates the novel, in ways conventional for tragedy. To give only one earlier example: Henchard forces the church choir at the Three Mariners to sing a Psalm as a curse against Farfrae, an ironic adumbration of the fact that the force of the curse comes to be applied against Henchard himself. Indeed, his own deathbed will is an echo of the Psalm's curse. What elsewhere might be a simple inversion of expectation is compacted by the doubled directorship of the narrative between Henchard and the narrator.

This coupled perspective of the narratorial situation has particular bearing for the portrayal of Henchard. It helps establish a 'realistic' assessment of his tragic stature, a blending of the transient moment and enduring implication.

Henchard may be 'mythic' and immense in personal force but his foibles and deep flaws in character counter the suggestion of a cosmic force working against him. His invoking a curse against Farfrae may immediately relieve Henchard's feelings but it also reveals that the universe (or moral system of poetic justice) opposes him, as signified by the pertinently 'splendid' symbolic gesture of the Psalm curse redounding upon the agent. Henchard himself accepts judgment against him; he willingly believes that 'a sinister intelligence' is 'bent on punishing him' by revealing Elizabeth-Jane's parentage (via Susan's letter). The emotional and aesthetic impact of the suggestion of the universe's enmity is unaffected by the narrator's rejection of the idea. In whatever fashion these various points may be incorporated into a reader's reaction, the drift of the narrator's presentation of Henchard is to enhance the loneliness of efforts to master himself within his changing situations.

As an isolate, Henchard makes a world for himself out of the world he enters but to which he feels no innate connection. Thus he veers to extremes because his conception of his self and its needs varies with the situation. His dissatisfaction with his situation attests his need to be the maker of his world rather than an abider in a world controlled by others. That he and Elizabeth-Jane seldom coincide in their affection for each other is *his* fault, not Elizabeth-Jane's, who is faithful until her climactic rejection -- when he has ceased to attempt to shape a world and only wants to return to one of his old ones.

This essay, however, does not intend to deal with Hardy's grander triumphs. What I am suggesting is that these large ambitions are justified by, and are consistent with, Hardy's attentions to what philosophically attuned readers would consider to be minor and modest. Hardy's achievements are far from small, but in the smallness of word-choice, the phrase, the individual passage, the modification of narrator perspective, lies the grounds for Hardy's permanent attractiveness as much as in the grandeur of Henchard's self-isolation. Profundity and austerity are made persuasive through confidence in the artist's attention to the small touch.

NOTES

1   Thomas Hardy, *The Life and Work of Thomas Hardy*, ed. Michael Millgate (London: Macmillan, 1985), pp. 185-86. Subsequent citations are parenthetical to *Life and Work*.

2   Thomas Hardy, *The Mayor of Casterbridge*, ed. Dale Kramer. The World's Classics Edition (Oxford: Oxford University Press, 1987), pp. 19-20. Subsequent citations are parenthetical.

Thomas Hardy: An Idiosyncratic Mode of Regard

Phillip Mallett

To begin with three characteristic passages from the *Life*:

(a) Reflecting on his experiences of the world so far as he had got he came to the conclusion that he did not wish to grow up. ...he did not want at all to be a man, or to possess things, but to remain as he was, in the same spot, and to know no more people than he already knew (about half a dozen).

(b) 'To think of life as passing away is a sadness; to think of it as past is at least tolerable. Hence even when I enter a room I have unconsciously the habit of regarding the scene as if I were a spectre not solid enough to influence my environment, only fit to behold and say, as another spectre said: "Peace be unto you".'

(c) An hour later one, going to his bedside yet again, saw on the death-face an expression such as she had never seen before on any being, or indeed on any presentment of the human countenance. Later the first radiance died away, but dignity and peace remained as long as eyes could see the mortal features of Thomas Hardy. [1]

The first of these passages had been anticipated in *Jude the Obscure*, where the young Jude reflects that he does not want to grow up in a world where 'Nature's logic' is so 'horrid' that kindness towards one set of creatures is cruelty towards another. To grow up is to discover himself at the 'centre' of his time rather than at a point on its circumference, and even to think of this movement from the margin to the centre produces in Jude 'a sort of shuddering', an existential nausea before the 'glaring, garish, rattling' experiences which threaten to shake and warp his life. In the event, the logic of society proves as cruel as that of Nature, and his dying words are an echo of Job's curses on the day wherein he was born. Deserted by Sue and by Arabella, lying within earshot of the Remembrance Games in Christminster, Jude dies alone, willing himself beyond even the circumference of his time. [2]

The second passage recalls Keats's discussion of the 'poetical Character'. In a letter to Woodhouse in 1818, Keats explained that when he was in company 'the identity of every one in the room begins [so] to press upon me that, I am in a very little time an[ni]hilated'. Yet this loss of identity is felt simultaneously as an enlargement, since it derives from the way the 'camelion Poet' is constantly 'in for [?informing] -- and filling some other Body'. [3] But where Keats writes of the self flowing into the being of others, Hardy's note suggests an instinctive refusal of self-identity. It was written in response to some remarks by Lady Ritchie, Thackeray's daughter and the sister-in-law of Leslie Stephen, who told Hardy that it was only through her children that she had any interest in the future; when she called on the Stephens she felt like a ghost, 'who arouses sad feelings in the person visited'. The Hardys, now in their late forties, had no children, and there was no obvious heir to the newly-built Max Gate. The role of the spectral observer is adopted to cope with the sense of time as passing away, or past, but not still to come. Rather than demanding more from life, to compensate for its inevitable transience, Hardy's response is to let it go, with a gentle blessing on those who, unlike himself, had expected much.

The first two passages are by Hardy, the ghost-writer of his own biography; the third was written by Florence soon after his death. The syntax of the first sentence is awkward, resulting in an unnerving hesitation before the 'one' who revisits 'his' bedside is identified as 'she'. The hesitation, like the diction -- presentment, death-face, radiance -- disturbingly echoes Hardy's own voice, as if Florence had caught her husband's habit of narrating events through the mediation of an anonymous, ghostly spectator, only putatively present. For a moment the 'one' who gazed on Hardy's death-face is allowed to become a 'she', but she remains unnamed, and the second sentence, with its unspecific 'as long as eyes could see', determinedly excludes her from the scene. Hardy's countenance, dignified but unseeing, is met by a gaze which belongs to no-one, or perhaps to everyone. [4]

To avoid growing up, possessing or knowing; to look on the lives of others as a disempowered spectre; to be, unseeing, the object of an unknown gaze. These passages seem to direct us, psychologically, to a willed self-suppression in Hardy, accompanied by a melancholy tenderness towards others. And yet tonally and stylistically each of them is markedly individual. Hardy disclaims our attention in a voice we are unlikely to mistake for that of any other writer, and which we have learned to call 'Hardyesque'. [5] The purpose of this essay is not, however, to explore Hardy's psychology. I want instead to look at some of the observers in Hardy's fiction, at what Hardy himself termed his 'idiosyncratic mode of regard'. [6] To that end I want to consider three novels which feature characters presented as observers, of varying degrees of reliability: *Far from the Madding Crowd*, *The Return of the Native*, and *The Mayor of Casterbridge*. In doing so, I want also to comment on the role of that narrative voice, at once distinctive and self-effacing, which seems so close to the Thomas Hardy described in the *Life*.

* * *

The opening chapter of *Far from the Madding Crowd* introduces us to Gabriel Oak and Bathsheba Everdene, the two characters who will still be present at the end of the novel. [7] Oak is the subject of a leisurely description. The voice of the first sentence is relaxed and superior ('When Farmer Oak smiled, the corners of his mouth spread till they were within an unimportant distance of his ears...'). and Oak's name, age, appearance, work, reputation, marital status, are all swiftly disclosed. While the narrator is presumably among those 'thoughtful persons' who can see beyond Gabriel's unassuming outward manner to his essential durability, he is clearly confident that the character of Farmer Oak will pose no problems of interpretation. [8]

Bathsheba's appearance follows, though she is not named until Chapter IV. Initially she is seen through Oak's eyes; the caged canary and the pot plants which surround her on the waggon are 'probably' from the windows of the house she has just vacated, which suggests Oak's guess rather than the narrator's authority. Bathsheba studies a package, then, believing herself unobserved, opens it, and 'a small looking-glass was disclosed'. The characteristic Hardy locution (not just 'she took out a looking-glass') reminds us that she is the object of scrutiny -- ours, and Gabriel's, and then her own, as she smiles into the glass. What follows shifts back and forth from certainty to doubt. The sunlight falls on her crimson jacket and dark hair, but 'what possessed her', whether her smile began as 'a factitious one, to test her capacity in that art', is hidden: 'nobody knows'. But 'it ended certainly in a real one', at which she blushes, and 'seeing her reflection blush, blushed the more'. The episode plays the intimacy of her delighted self-absorption against the baffled curiosity of spectator and reader alike. The commentary seems weighed down with the narrator's authority: 'The picture was a delicate one. Woman's prescriptive infirmity had stalked into the sunlight...'. This is hardly Gabriel's voice, but he too draws a 'cynical inference' from the scene, despite his willingness to be generous towards a handsome girl. Bathsheba's actions have no purpose that he can understand: 'she simply observed herself as a fair product of Nature in the feminine kind.' The narrator and Oak appear to agree. But when her thoughts seem 'to glide into far-off though likely dramas' of men's hearts lost and won, the narrator abruptly withdraws: 'this was but conjecture.' The whole series of actions was performed so casually 'as to make it rash to assert that intention had any part in them at all'. No inference, whether cynical or generous, is to be drawn. Bathsheba's thoughts are inaccessible to the narrator, as to Oak, and also therefore to the reader.

This unsettling effect is repeated at the end of the chapter, when Oak pays twopence to the turnpike-keeper to allow the waggon through, and Bathsheba dismisses him with scarcely a glance. Later, of course, she will need his help to pass through harder barriers than this, and he will make himself a kind of mirror in which she has to see herself, not in warm sunlight, as here, but 'in the cold morning light of open-shuttered disillusion' (140-41). The last word of the chapter, 'Vanity' -- the short name for 'Women's prescriptive infirmity' -- is his, but he is 'perhaps a little piqued' by Bathsheba's indifference. The judgment the narrator had seemed to endorse, by suggesting that 'we all know' how women respond to the kind of favour Oak has done, is now ascribed to Oak's wounded pride, and the narrator remains non-committal, even, for the moment, about Oak himself ('perhaps'). Scrutiny, speculation, generalisation, have all failed to explain Bathsheba. The privacy on which the reader has broken is in a sense restored to her.

This variety of angles of vision produces a number of effects. First, it dramatises one of the issues of the novel: the attempt by three different men to impose an identity -- and their own name -- on Bathsheba. Here she is allowed to elude the efforts of both Oak and the narrator to intercept her self-contemplation, and to reduce her smiles and blushes to familiar maxims about female vanity. Second, it alerts us to what the novel will *not* be. It will not be an account of the heroine's gradual development towards a position of wisdom embodied in Oak and endorsed by the narrator. The novel is not stable in that way, and the relationship between Oak, the narrator and the reader continues to change. Manifestly Oak exhibits many qualities we are invited to admire, but that is not to make him the moral centre of the novel, or at any rate not its sole moral centre. Right or wrong in his advice to Bathsheba, he remains unresponsive to aspects of her nature: those, for example, which draw her towards Sergeant Troy. Oak is not offered as a fully adequate 'register' or guide to our reading of her character.

The changing angle of vision has another effect. Taken with the narrator's willingness to withdraw from judgment, it at least tends towards a view of woman-as-enigma. Bathsheba looking into her mirror is a 'picture', a 'scene', offered to us to read. [9] That we are baffled testifies to Hardy's readiness to acknowledge her autonomy, but we remain voyeurs, examining a woman as an image, a sign to be interpreted, rather than an agent in her own life. Hardy is sympathetic to the distress which prompts Bathsheba's comment to Boldwood, that 'It is difficult for a woman to define her feelings in language, which is chiefly made by men to express theirs' (364), but is yet unsure how, as a male narrator, he can observe, describe, and make speak, a woman. Later novels return to the problem; here it is recognised, if only tacitly, in the refusal to assume an authoritative view of his heroine, but it is not resolved. [10]

* * *

It is natural to associate the narrative voice in the first chapter of *The Return of the Native* with the passages quoted above from the *Life*. The narrator here is similarly self-effacing, a spectator who seems powerless to influence the world he describes, and almost to deny his presence as an observer of the heath: 'A Saturday afternoon in November was approaching the time of twilight, and the vast tract of unenclosed wild known as Egdon Heath embrowned itself moment by moment.' [11] Time and place are mentioned, but not persons; it is only in the second chapter that 'Humanity appears on the scene'. The date too is unspecific. The Victorian novel typically establishes a gap between the events of the story and the time of reading, which allows the reassuring suggestion that the story has become part of what makes our present, and in the process has been accommodated, absorbed into it. This chapter does not offer that reassurance. Instead, the sense of time shifts, from this one Saturday afternoon to a generalised present: 'The place became full of a watchful intentness now' -- every day, at this time, as Egdon begins 'its nightly roll into darkness', but also on this particular day, as the heath starts to 'awake' and 'listen'. 'Now' is not a date, but the moment when Egdon tells its 'true tale', and awakes to listen to its own narrative, as if to learn whether the story that follows is just one of many, or the forerunner of 'the final overthrow' it seems to await. In doing so, it effectively supplants the narrator, as the disembodied voice which broods over the scene is reduced to the vehicle through which Egdon tells its story. 'It would have been noticed that ... the white surface of the road remained as clear as ever': would have been, that is, had there been someone there to observe it. The white road opens at the end of the first chapter to allow humanity to appear, the dark waters of Shadwater Weir finally close over two of its representatives. Like other tellers of tales, the heath reveals its character in its story; it has, to use the terms of Hardy's General Preface (1912) one of those natures which 'become vocal at tragedy'. It has 'a lonely face, suggesting tragical possibilities'; it exhales darkness; it is the original of our 'midnight dreams of flight and disaster' -- precisely what it offers, at the close of the story, with the suicide of Eustacia.

Two kinds of effect follow from the way the narrative voice yields to that of Egdon. First, it suggests that the story will have some of the heath's own grandeur or 'sublimity'; it won't be 'commonplace, unmeaning, nor tame'. Unlike Emma Bovary, whom she in some ways resembles, Eustacia will not become 'vulgar' on Egdon. Despite her hostility to it, she takes her colouring from the heath, at times almost literally, as her 'smouldering rebelliousness' and her black hair and dress seem to repeat the reddle beneath the dark surface of the turf. Living in Budmouth or Paris as Wildeve's mistress, Eustacia would have lost her grandeur; drowned on Egdon Heath, her beauty at last finds 'an artistically happy background' (381). The familiar 'observer' would even have felt that Wildeve was 'born for a higher destiny'. There is here a kind of promise that the story will repay the reader's fullest and most committed emotional response. But this sublime story, in harmony with the heath, will also be a tragic one. For a second effect of the opening chapter is to suggest that failure -- flight and disaster -- is the absolute and unchallengeable ground of our being, and, accordingly, that the aspiration and rebellion shown by Clym and Eustacia will be exercised in vain. If so, the reader's emotional investment will be betrayed, because their story, like the other stories told on Egdon, will 'make little impression'. Eustacia's longing for passionate love, Clym's ambition to bring education to Egdon Heath, will be defeated. As Lawrence put it in his *Study of Thomas Hardy* (1914), 'the question of their unfortunate end is begged in the beginning'. [12]

Lawrence's essay, conceived, written and re-written while he was working on *The Rainbow*, is as much an argument with Nietzsche and Tolstoy, and with himself, as it is an account of Hardy's fiction, but he does suggest a serious criticism of *The Return of the Native*. Various critics have read the novel as showing Clym's laudable desire to serve his fellow-men brought to ruin by Eustacia. Others have seen it as showing how Eustacia's passionate desire for 'what is called life' -- her Paterian wish 'to burn always with this hard, gemlike flame, this ecstasy' -- is denied and thwarted by Clym. [13] Might it be, then, that Hardy uses each character to limit the other? Eustacia's first appearance encourages us to expect that the novel will turn away from the communal bonfire, to follow her Promethean yearnings, her solitary bonfire, illicit passion, and desire for grandeur. Timothy Fairways, Grandfer Cantle and the rest seem to represent the mean and commonplace, men and women whose highest ambition is to come through life unscathed, and whose morality is more or less fairly reflected in the traditional values of the mumming and the maypole. We can hardly expect that these will be the values of the novel. But Eustacia's death by slow degrees in the role of Turkish Knight at the mumming proves to foreshadow her gradual submission to the steady and unsympathetic pressure their world exerts on her, while Clym, initially the proponent of high thinking and the love of wisdom, appears in Book V of the novel as the last and cruellest agent of this morality -- the St. George of Egdon Heath. On this reading, Hardy is unwilling to make the commitment to his central characters that is their due, and fails the reader by retreating from the hard task of imagining success for them. The image of the heath, suggesting the futility of all human ambition, is used as an excuse for a failure of moral and imaginative nerve not in the characters, but in the novelist. [14]

This is at best an incomplete reading. The spectral observer who gives way to the 'watchful intentness' of the heath also makes room for more prosaic observers of it: the hypothetical furze-cutter, for whom its darkness merely complicates the question of what time to stop work; an antiquarian, who has researched various 'intelligible facts' in the Domesday Book, and knows the history and the Latin name (*Turbaria Bruaria*) of the charters relating to the right of cutting turf from the heath; and another, sociologically-minded, who speculates on the future of tourism with all the judiciousness of a *Saturday Reviewer* ('The time seems near, if it has not actually arrived ...'). These other observers represent the 'civilisation' which is Egdon's 'enemy'. Instead of yielding to the heath, they encroach upon it. They imply not the inevitability of defeat but the possibility of work, records, investigations, leisure. Their world, the world of the road rather than the barrow, is neither tragic nor sublime. Nor, however, is it to be despised. The first chapter of the novel is, in fact, indeterminate about the ground of our being. The disembodied voice of the opening paragraph, which it is tempting to identify with the Thomas Hardy who didn't want to grow up, who wanted to look on life as a spectre, intuits tragedy as an absolute; darkness is our 'true tale', and our failure and defeat are inescapable, even though our resistance may be grand. The other observers -- the furze-cutter, the antiquarian, and so on -- cautiously and moderately occupy the heath, and come together into a community. What this suggests is that even in the first pages of an ambitiously tragic novel Hardy was anxious to let the voice and values of the community emerge as one element, and not a negligible one, of the whole. No doubt the attempt owes something to his own temperament, and something too to Shakespeare's tragedies, where porters, clowns and gravediggers share the stage with kings, queens and princes. The message is that of Brueghel's picture of Icarus falling from the sky, as Auden describes it in 'Musée des Beaux Arts'

> how everything turns away
> Quite leisurely from the disaster; the ploughman may
> Have heard the splash, the forsaken cry,
> But for him it was not an important failure; the sun shone
> As it had to on the white legs disappearing into the green
> Water.

Nonetheless, it is difficult not to feel that rather than holding together in a single fiction the tragic and the everyday, Hardy's novel veers from one to the other, from the Promethean aspirations of Clym and Eustacia to the domestic world of those who have learned to mend and make do. In this first chapter, the alternative to the sublime is said to be the 'commonplace', but in Chapter 7 ('The Queen of the Night') the antithesis is re-phrased, in terms more tolerant of the mundane and unheroic: 'To have lost the godlike conceit that we may do what we will, and not to have acquired a homely zest for doing what we can, shows a grandeur of temper which ... if congenial to philosophy, is apt to be dangerous to the commonwealth' (68). Here sublimity is re-named conceit, and the commonplace is re-read as the homely -- a word which for Hardy has always a strong positive resonance. But this seems still further to disavow the Prometheanism which marks Clym and Eustacia. So far as the heath writes its narrative in the form of tragedy, it at least allows the central characters their grandeur, but there is also a suggestion in the first chapter that its preferred form might be 'satire': immediately, on human vanity in wearing brightly-coloured clothes, but more generally, on the desire to be exceptional, to seek fulfilment as an individual rather than as a member of the commonwealth. The oddity of *The Return of the Native* is that it is both a tragic and an anti-tragic novel, both celebration of and satire on the demand for 'what is called life'.

This uncertainty of tone and direction is felt elsewhere in the novel. The first chapter implies an observer of the heath, and explores Egdon's own 'watchful intentness'. The second presents another, equally watchful: Diggory Venn. Diggory provides a typically equivocal point of entry into the narrative. He is at first himself the object of observation; Captain Vye looks back to see him on the road, and 'the natural query of an observer' would have been to ask why he had given himself up to his trade -- a question never fully answered. When Venn stops to rest his ponies and looks up at Rainbarrow, the novel follows his 'traveller's eye'. But when the figure of Eustacia is seen on top of the barrow we are told that 'the first instinct of an imaginative stranger' would be to think of the ancient Celts, and this is not Venn's role; nor, when she departs, and 'the imagination of the observer clung by preference to that vanished, solitary figure', can we suppose that this refers to Venn, who is not interested in Eustacia, nor in anyone except Thomasin. We find, in fact, an echo of the dichotomies of the opening chapter: a tired traveller, occupied with Thomasin's domestic sorrows, and an imaginative brooding observer, who will follow Eustacia's story, and who waits for her on top of Rainbarrow after the other heath-dwellers have gone down to the Quiet Woman Inn.

Venn's role as observer adds greatly to the complexity of the novel. Hardy introduces him partly because he is of antiquarian interest, a 'curious' link with 'obsolete forms of life', introduced in the novel because, as Hardy says in the 1912 Preface, 'things were like that in Wessex'.But evidently Venn is given his employment because of the associations it attracts. As well as being curious, he is also 'isolated' and 'weird', and was of course originally intended to remain so. The associations that gather round him make him virtually the *genius loci* of the heath. It too is described as 'obsolete', and Venn lives in its hollows (Johnny Nunsuch tumbles into one); it is 'Ishmaelitish', reddlemen are linked with Cain; buried beneath its turves to spy on Wildeve and Eustacia, he enacts its 'watchful intentness'. The 'blood-coloured figure' of the reddleman is also the original of our dreams, 'the sublimation of all the horrid dreams which had afflicted the juvenile spirit since imagination began'. His, too if a face on which time seems to make little impression; he sits silently in the Quiet Woman Inn, unseen till the last, and plays his game of dice impassively, like an 'automaton'. Blood-coloured or fire-coloured, it is he who brings to life as events in the plot the energy hidden behind the apparent repose of the heath.

Like the heath, he seems to require different and opposing responses. On one level, he is merely the lover of Thomasin, in his own way 'slighted and enduring', and resolved to protect her happiness, even if that means keeping Wildeve at home with her, and himself therefore on the margins of her life. In pursuit of this goal he is indifferent to what happens to anyone else. On another level, he is the catalyst or trigger for a series of disasters and misfortunes. He offers to Mrs. Yeobright to re-assume his role as Thomasin's suitor, but that only stimulates Wildeve's interest in Eustacia, which Venn wishes to reduce. He tries to restore Thomasin's guineas after the gambling scene on the heath, but his error in sending none to Clym frustrates Mrs. Yeobright's effort to heal the breach between her and her son. His 'rough coercion' deters Wildeve from visiting Eustacia at night, but only persuades him to call during the day; consequently Wildeve is present when Mrs. Yeobright calls, Eustacia is afraid to open the door, and Mrs. Yeobright is forced to turn back across the heath. He tells Clym that his mother was making a would-be friendly visit, and thus sets in train the suspicions which lead to Eustacia's departure. Benignly intentioned -- towards Thomasin -- Venn is in fact pivotal first in preparing Eustacia to love Clym, then in pushing her back towards Wildeve, and finally in her bitter separation from her husband. In these ways he embodies all that seems irrational in the nature of things, unamenable or resistant to the human will: those chances which we feel as malign, even though we conscientiously regard them as merely natural or indifferent. He thus comes to personify the incongruity between human desire and purpose on the one hand, and on the other the realities of frustration and defeat, which is so much a part of Hardy's imaginative world. We might call him, in Hardy's own terms, a 'purblind doomster'. [15]

To see Venn as epitomising the casually cross-purposed character of our lives is to pull the novel away from Eustacia's sense of the world as 'fearfully malignant'. This, at least, is where we are led if we attend to Venn's deeds and actions, that is, to the plot of the novel. If, however, we allow the emphasis in reading to fall on his 'sinister redness', and on the images which link him with the heath, Eustacia's cry, 'O, the cruelty of putting me into this, ill-conceived world!', seems more nearly justified. [16] That the firelight from Susan Nunsuch's house lights her like 'a figure in a phantasmagoria' recalls the lurid and sinister lights associated with his presence; similarly, Susan's raking aside the 'dark and dead' ashes of her turf fire to reveal 'a glow of red heat' underneath, as she melts her wax image of Eustacia, suggests his concealment of himself, red beneath the turves, to spy on her lovemaking with Wildeve (355, 361). The suggestion that she seems 'drawn into the Barrow by a hand from beneath' disturbingly recalls his living in its hollows (358). Mrs. Yeobright is doubtful about Wildeve's mistake over the wedding-license: 'Such things don't happen for nothing' (41). The remark can be turned against her, in connection with her error in entrusting the money for her estranged son to, of all people, Christian Cantle. Both her error and Wildeve's may reflect an unadmitted hostile intention. On a realist reading of the novel, Venn cannot have intended the results his interventions achieve -- the destruction of three people, including Eustacia, who stand between him and Thomasin. But the highly charged language of the novel, and the instability of the narrative point of view, suggest that Hardy was not committed to writing as a realist. Venn's presence as an agent in Eustacia's life, indifferent towards her, and not understanding of her -- his eye is not 'trained' enough to see her beauty -- helps maintain the double perspective on the events of the novel: both romantic tragedy, and satire on human aspiration.

Book VI of the novel shows Venn returned to his former self. However it was wrung from him, Hardy allowed the revised ending of the novel to stand for fifty years, so we must make what we can of it -- though his suggestion that readers with a more severe artistic code could reject it is in keeping with the wider indeterminacy of the novel. It is Book VI, presumably, which has encouraged so many critics to see Venn as a solid citizen or yeoman. He does, at least, return to the 'commonwealth' of those who do with a 'homely zest' what they can; his marriage to Thomasin is a comic apotheosis to answer the tragic deaths of Book V. The end of the novel thus continues to allow various views to lie alongside each other. The sublime may also be 'godlike conceit', the 'commonplace' may be another name for the values of the 'commonwealth'; Venn is an agent of all that is alien in the heath, but also a rejected lover who brings into focus ordinary human error and miscalculation. Barbara Hardy, in *The Appropriate Form* (1964), speaks of what she calls 'the dogmatic form' of

Hardy's novels. What this reading of *The Return of the Native* suggests is that this is precisely what Hardy's forms are not. The varying points of view in the novel, the refusal to suggest that the narrator is the kind of unitary being we encounter in, say, George Eliot, and the ambiguities associated with Diggory Venn, underline the way conflicting responses to the novel's material -- plot, character, world view -- are here left unresolved.

* * *

Gabriel Oak and Diggory Venn have often been seen to have much in common: the sterling virtues of patience and durability, to those who see them as agents of order in the community; a tendency to spy on others, and to be morally censorious towards the passionate woman who in some way resists them, to those less sympathetic. Their resemblance to another figure, Elizabeth-Jane in *The Mayor of Casterbridge*, seems not to have been discussed, but there are striking similarities. They are all three thrifty individuals, who have learned to live in 'the rear of opportunity'. [17] Like Oak, comfortably eating bacon that has been dropped on the road by not quite letting his teeth meet (' 'tis wonderful what can be done by contrivance'), Elizabeth-Jane knows 'the secret ... of making limited opportunities endurable' (334). They all suffer setbacks: Oak is reduced from farmer to shepherd, Venn to supplying reddle, Elizabeth-Jane to serving at table in the Three Mariners Inn. All three are at first rejected by their future partners, and all have to accept their role as the second spouse, taken up only after the first has proved in some way feckless or unreliable. At the same time, their marriages allow them to move up in the social scale, as they in turn supplant the rival who had supplanted them. They are all three censorious, especially towards women; Elizabeth-Jane is almost 'vicious' in her demand for propriety (216). They are hostile to those who challenge the 'commonwealth', and either mistrust or misunderstand the demand for individual fulfilment. They share what in *The Return of the Native* Clym is said not to possess, a 'well-proportioned mind'. The usual blessings of such a mind are 'happiness and mediocrity'; the rewards, in effect, of the ordinary, non-tragic world. [18]

Diggory Venn and Gabriel Oak are both observers, but far more than they are Elizabeth-Jane is used as a reliable witness, almost a surrogate narrator. At the same time, however, the drift of the novel is away from her way of seeing. Her viewpoint is never rejected, but it is revealed to be limited, and it is also at odds with the main narrative voice of the novel. This voice, as one comes to expect with Hardy, is itself a compound of different voices, ranging from what one might call an outer voice, remote from the action of the novel, to an inner one, closely informed by, and moved by, the events it discloses. Most removed is the voice of the Wessex commentator in those footnotes added in 1912

27

remarking on the physical changes to the town of Casterbridge ('Most of these old houses have now been pulled down' (31)). Somewhat closer stands the familiar putative observer, occasionally a direct observer, for example that figure who might have been on the road at the beginning of the novel alongside Henchard, Susan and their baby daughter, informed enough to identify the tools the man is carrying, skilfully reading the signs that bespeak an 'obviously long journey', but not able to interpret them fully: 'nobody but himself could have said precisely' what was the reason for Henchard's moody silence (6).

The immediate effect of this use of the observer is to suggest that we are reading an historical narrative, not a fiction. Our knowledge of events and motives is conditioned by what happens to have come down to us by report, and there are inevitably gaps in the record. But Hardy uses his observer in a variety of ways. At times he is compelled to be reticent: for example, what Lucetta revealed to Farfrae of her past following the skimmington-ride 'cannot be told', and must remain Farfrae's 'secret' -- though a few pages later it appears that 'Lucetta had confessed everything', an inconsistency which presumably did not trouble Hardy (288-89, 300). This reticence perhaps excuses what we might otherwise feel is improper dealing on Hardy's part, the comment in Chapter III that 'a glance was sufficient to inform the eye that [Elizabeth-Jane] was Susan Henchard's grown-up daughter' (21); although Henchard looks at her 'critically' when she risks wearing a brighter ribbon than usual, and Farfrae and others notice her 'budding beauty', it is not until chapter XIX that Henchard studies her face while she is asleep, and gradually detects the features of Newson (88, 96). But at other times the observer gives way to a narrator who possesses a significant foreknowledge. He is aware, as an observer could not be, that the quarrel between Henchard and Farfrae over the treatment of Abel Whittle is 'the seed that was to lift the foundation of this friendship', and that Farfrae is mistaken in thinking that there is 'no danger' in sitting down in Lucetta's drawing-room (97, 158). Crucially, the narrator knows, long before the facts are disclosed in Susan's letter, that Elizabeth-Jane is not Henchard's natural daughter. When Henchard comments on Elizabeth-Jane's colouring, Susan reacts with an 'uneasy expression', to which, the narrator comments, 'the future held the key' (90). The narrator, too, holds this key, and watches events in the full knowledge of how they will develop.

It is from this position of foreknowledge that the narrator, knowing what Henchard's fate is to be -- that there will be no rejoicing in heaven over this repentant sinner (286) -- can share Henchard's anguished sense that his every effort to make amends is in vain. And it is this sympathy with Henchard that drives the narrator to those generalisations about the 'ironical sequence of things' (127), the 'contrarious inconsistencies' of life (319), which Henchard too is impelled to make. It is the narrator's voice, as the Latinate diction suggests, that reflects on 'the ingenious machinery contrived by the gods for reducing human possibilities of amelioration to a minimum' (320), but he comes close here to Henchard's experience, and close to endorsing his view of the world. Usually the narrator conscientiously refuses to go as far as Henchard; when the latter feels he is being persecuted by events, the narrator explains that 'they had developed naturally', according to the usual laws of cause and effect (127). At other times he suggests that Henchard falls victim not to an external moral order, but to a self-destructive element in his own nature. We may perhaps read this as an instance of Henchard's fetishism, an unconscious attempt to internalise a moral order which might otherwise allow him to remain unpunished, and to 'castigate himself with the thorns which these restitutory acts brought in their train' (84). But increasingly the narrator's comments suggest a sympathy with Henchard's view. Henchard sees himself as justly punished for violating the moral order, the narrator sees him as punished to excess, and protests against that order as harsh and unjust. The allusions in the text to Cain, Saul, Job and Oedipus serve to remind us that others have felt the same need to protest.

But this is not the way Elizabeth-Jane sees the world. From the beginning of the novel we are encouraged to accept her role as an observer. Serving in the Three Mariners Inn, she sees 'without herself particularly being seen', and when she looks down on Henchard's yard, or on the Casterbridge market, she does so as a trustworthy witness (51). Her 'quiet eye' detects the nature of Henchard's relationship with Farfrae (91). She is a 'silent observing woman', who studies herself in the mirror to see how she is to be seen, wanting to know how Farfrae will react to her looks -- and she gets it right (112-13). She is described as a 'dumb, deep-feeling, great-eyed creature', who can be trusted to 'read' correctly the facts 'printed large' on Lucetta's face, or on those of Henchard and Farfrae as they compete for Lucetta's attention (133). She is even a 'discerning silent witch', who can remain indoors yet still see -- correctly, as it proves -- how Lucetta and Farfrae will behave together (172). Much of the narrative is thus communicated to us through her eyes. There are no suggestions, as there are with Oak and Venn, that she lacks insight. But her powers are limited in two ways. First, she does not know her own origins: whether she is Elizabeth Henchard or Elizabeth Newson. Second, she does not have the narrator's knowledge of the future. Her attention is focussed on the immediate issues of how to live: noting, for example, that Farfrae is respectable, that he has gone to the Three Mariners, and that the same inn will probably suit her and her mother. Rather than the almost disabling foreknowledge of the narrator, she has foresight, in the sense of prudence. She reads faces and events, and adapts to them, moving with small, provisional steps into each new situation -- in this, of course, the reverse of Henchard, whose character, like his business, moves in 'jolts' (91).

Hardy is scrupulously fair to Elizabeth-Jane as an observer. Her patience commands his respect, and that of the reader. And yet no more than Gabriel Oak or Diggory Venn is she a fully adequate register of events and character. Her response to Henchard's last days is surely too muted for us to feel it satisfactory. She carries out the wishes expressed in his will, knowing that they are 'not to be tampered with to give herself a mournful pleasure', but we miss her anger on his behalf: 'there's no altering -- so it must be' (333-34). But at the same time, if she is not moved to passion, she is moved to compassion. Elizabeth-Jane has learned to guard against the 'unforeseen', and to pursue an 'equable serenity' in an inequitable world. The closing paragraphs of the novel exhibit no protest on behalf of one exceptional man, but rather a generalised sense that a protest might be lodged on behalf of every man: 'neither she nor any human being deserved less than was given' (334). This is non-heroic, and non-tragic. It is not a view which should be too readily dismissed as insufficient; it is, after all, not very far from Hardy's own sense that his only comment on a world he could not control should be 'Peace be unto you'. But it is not a response open to the narrator who has stood so much closer to Michael Henchard, and who is still moved by the pain of his particular lot. Yet neither response is allowed entirely to override the other. In *The Return of the Native* two kinds of vision, one engrossed by the tragic elements in our experience, the other attentive to the domestic pleasures of daily life, are felt as antithetical, and the narrative voice seems unresolved between them, unsure whether to endorse or to mock Eustacia's demands for 'what is called life'. Promethean and anti-Promethean feelings jostle awkwardly against each other. In *The Mayor*, the two kinds of vision are again allowed to lie side by side, but here the conflict is not within the narrator, but between the narrator and Elizabeth-Jane. Like the earlier novel, it ends with a marriage and a death, but without the sense that these belong to different moral worlds. *The Mayor of Casterbridge*, more than any other of Hardy's books, is a tragic novel which finds room for the non-tragic view of life. It is one of his greatest achievements.

NOTES

1   Thomas Hardy, *The Life and Work of Thomas Hardy*, edited by Michael Millgate (London, 1984), pp. 20, 218, 481.

2   *Jude the Obscure*, edited by Patricia Ingham (Oxford, 1985), p. 13.

3   *Letters of John Keats: a new selection*, edited by Robert Gittings (Oxford, 1970), p. 157.

4   The 'she' was in fact Eva Dugdale. The draft of this chapter perhaps links the dying Hardy still more closely with Jude: a cancelled passage records that 'a few broken sentences, one of these heartrending in its poignancy, showed that his mind had reverted to a sorrow of the past' (*Life and Work*, p. 543). In *Thomas Hardy: a Biography* (Oxford, 1982), Michael Millgate points out that Florence was downstairs at the moment of death, 'and it is not clear that any such sentences were ever spoken' (p. 572, note). I don't understand this note, since it leaves unexplained why the sentences were ever recorded in Florence's draft. It is easy to see why they were removed, but not why they were written, unless they were accurate.

5 The paradox is repeated in the poems, for example in 'Afterwards', and in 'I have lived with shades', where we read, after the poet's death, his own prophecy that he will not survive:

He moves me not at all;
I note no ray or jot
Of rareness in his lot,
Or star exceptional.
  Into the dim
  Dead throngs around
  He'll sink, nor sound
  Be left of him.
-- except, of course, the sound of this and other poems.

6 *Life and Work*, p. 235. On p. 245 Hardy records that he was thinking of 'A Bird's-Eye View of Europe at the beginning of the nineteenth century', and on p. 246 that 'If I were a painter I would paint a picture of a room as viewed by a mouse from a chink under the skirting'. It is entirely characteristic that Hardy should consider both a bird's-eye and a mouse's-eye view in this way.

7 References to *Far from the Madding Crowd* are to the edition by Suzanne B. Falck-Yi, with an introduction by Simon Gattrell (Oxford, 1993), and except where otherwise indicated to the first chapter of the novel.

8 This need not suggest, though Rosemarie Morgan makes out a convincing case in *Cancelled Words* (London and New York, 1992), that because 'Oak demands very little of Hardy's revising pen' (p. 66) the novelist himself lacked interest in Gabriel's character.

9 This issue is more widely discussed in Patricia Ingham, *Thomas Hardy* (London, 1989); see especially chapter 2, 'Women as Signs in the Early Novels'.

10 I have argued this more fully in 'Sexual Ideology and Narrative Form in *Jude the Obscure*,' in *English*, XXXVIII (Autumn, 1989).

11 References to *The Return of the Native* are to the edition by Simon Gattrell (Oxford, 1990), and except where otherwise indicated to the first two chapters of the novel.

12 D. H. Lawrence, *Study of Thomas Hardy*, in *Lawrence on Hardy & Painting*, edited with an introduction by J. V. Davies (London, 1973), p. 51.

13 Merryn Williams, in *Thomas Hardy and Rural England* (London, 1972), is among those sympathetic to Clym; Rosemarie Morgan, in *Women and Sexuality in the Novels of Thomas Hardy* (London, 1988), makes the case for Eustacia.

14 Richard Swigge, in *Lawrence, Hardy, and American Literature* (Oxford, 1972) ,develops Lawrence's arguments with considerable force; see especially pp. 4-13.

15 See Hardy's poem 'Hap': 'These purblind Doomsters had as readily strown / Blisses about my pilgrimage as pain.'

16 *The Return of the Native*, p. 359. This is the reading in the 1895 and all subsequent editions; in 1878 Eustacia described the world as 'imperfect' as well as 'ill-conceived'. The 1895 text is sharper.

17 *The Mayor of Casterbridge*, edited by Dale Kramer (Oxford, 1972), p. 88. Subsequent references to this edition are given parenthetically in the text.

18 The references in this paragraph are to *Far from the Madding Crowd*, p. 60, and *The Return of the Native*, p. 175.

Mothering the Text: Hardy's Vanishing Maternal Abode

Rosemarie Morgan

Hardy was a much haunted man. He remained deeply attached to spectres, phantoms and even 'Shadows of beings who fellowed with myself of earlier days'; shadows of selves that merge with other selves, that verge on other existences with such intensity that 'I seem where I was before my birth, and after death may be'. [1]

Such attachments are familiar enough to readers of the poems, although they are prosaically muted in the *Life*. Here the autobiographical self itself intends to vanish, or at any rate conjures a ghost-writer: a (presumed) female biographer. In this sense, Hardy's autobiographical self becomes schematically detached from its own past, and from most past natal attachments, by means of pseudonymous authorship. Somewhere between haunted poet and disappearing autobiographer comes the novelist. Less obsessively, if rather more problematically -- in terms of resurrecting the vanished world of natal origins -- the Wessex novels aspire to a reunion with the past which is fraught with conflicting desires to find and lose, to hold and let go, to recover and abandon, and even to put life itself into reverse. Hardy authorises this world, 'fathers' it with his own creations, but in the dual sense that he is born from it and yearns to conserve his original attachment to it (extending into it, for example, both his mother's and grandmother's stories), the more telling phrase seems to me to be 'mothering'. 'Telling', though, is also apt in so far as it not only matches the epistemological considerations outlined above -- the ancestral 'voices', the 'telling' voices coming down from the maternal side of the homeland story -- but it also matches 'mothering the text' to thematics, to the Wessex *telos*, to the heartbreak in it.

Thematically, in returning the 'native' to the natal land, yet in missing (in all senses of the word) a complete reunion with the past, the Wessex story reiterates the primal curse of expulsion. We begin with this. Our story, at the moment of birth, begins with expulsion. The 'mothering' body (in sexual and textual reproduction alike), generates a series of difficult, forcible detachments -- from the womb, from the maternal breast, and ultimately (at puberty -- instinctually if not ideologically), from the intimate threshhold of the nurturing body itself. I speak, then, of Hardy's act of 'mothering the text' not simply because he invokes a variety of narrative forms that manifest ambivalent desires to recreate and lose abodes of the past, or that recreate and abandon the beloved (lost, young mother of infancy) in scenes that repeat the motif of unattainability, or that bring forth new life from buried origins, or that reproduce (homeland, natal landscapes) scenic forms that are spatially continuous with life. I use it to draw attention to the fact that one of the fundamental motifs central to the Wessex chronicle makes manifest many of these desires in the most primal of terms: the desire to repossess the lost nurturing body. The Wessex construct itself, as the imaginative reconstruction of the country of origins, literally and figuratively embodies that desire. [2]

* * *

To begin with a rather rudimentary narrative act of forcible detachment, simply at the surface-text level, we have Hardy's method of displacing his narrator from the world-in-view. Most readers of the Wessex novels are familiar enough with that aspect of contingency, in Hardy's relationship to the past, which seems to compel him to invite parties of bystander narrators to comment on what 'might have been', what 'may have come', or what 'could have been'. Depending on the type of guest narrator invited in -- humourist, pessimist, ironist, misanthropist, historicist, cynicist, misogynist -- the scene, event, character or action will instantly reflect the new point of view and, rather startlingly, will reflect it in a mode of regard as often as not utterly *regardless* of pre-existing modes.

Practised readers perceive these interceptions as purposive modes of narrative unsettlement -- as in establishing textual indeterminacy or tropic devices for 'making strange'. It suffices, here, that these voices utter themselves as nameless, faceless disembodied presences who unsettle time-present by pushing in with time-past. A kind of temporal riddle then occurs. Specifically, as in the use of the conditional tense (a bystander 'could have' or 'would have observed'), an obsolete past pushes up against a wished-for futurity. The sense of riddled time is intensified by the fact that the bystander narrator rarely belongs in the present world, the world-in-view, the action afoot. So, in effect, each visitant brings in another 'time' (as indicated by Hardy's shift to the conditional tense), another dimension -- a differing point of view -- and remains invisible to the other characters. Events are not touched in any way by their presence. Even Hardy's primary narrator may not know who they are, or at best, may know them only by indefinition, by the indefinite article, as in the opening of *The Return of the Native* where we meet a typically commonplace visitant and are told:

Looking upwards, a furze-cutter would have been inclined to continue work; looking down, he would have decided to finish his faggot and go home.

As like as not our furze-cutter would have done neither of these things. Not a *Hardyan* furze-cutter, not a furze-cutter who belonged in this world. After all, the heath is flat, dull and vacant, with a dry, white road stretching across it, and along this road a rather picturesque old man (clearly of keen interest to the primary narrator) is at this very moment walking very deliberately, and as he walks he draws nearer and nearer to a speck in the distance which turns out to be a van -- and a very odd-looking van at that. Is there a labourer in the entire universe of Wessex who would not -- 'looking upwards' at this point -- shoulder his burden and trundle across the heath to nose into this scene, or creep up on it with casual indifference, or hide behind the furze to spy on it?

None of this happens, of course. Our 'furze-cutter' is knowable only to the primary narrator and Hardy's reader. Yet, in these instances of perspectival shift, more notably where the new presence casts an alien judgement upon the scene (as when a Grundyist stops by to denigrate the heroine), the primary narrator is forcibly displaced. While this does, on occasion, severely rupture the coherency of the text, its very consistency of technique points to something closely resembling a notational device whereby the reader is alerted to crises of (textual) dislocation. It happens in triadic form. First, the text is 'conditioned', so to speak, by the temporal discontinuity of the verbal shift to the conditional tense. Then there is the perspectival discontinuity occasioned by the bystander commentator. And, finally, there is the momentary crisis: the displacement of the primary narrator.

We do not have to reach far into Hardy's world, from this small point of momentary 'casting out', to find increasingly larger parallels of alienation, dislocation, broken continuities and lost horizons intersecting the *weltan-schauung* of his reconstructed homeland. There are, of course, the tragic tales themselves, in which life cannot go on for those who find themselves out of place in the world. Then too there is the march of progress, the new displacing the old -- although compared with many of his Victorian peers, Hardy seems relatively untroubled by the onrush of change and industrialisation. Was he, perhaps, safeguarded by his remarkable sense of the past's spatial continuity with life? Was this the enabling power that led him to experience the world of prehistoric antiquity as no less imediate for the fact that it may be overlaid by railroads? 'Immediate', not so much because it yields up its palpable artefacts, its stones, fossils and bones, but because these themselves yield up vital essences, animistic presences.

True, we are back again with the haunted man. But with this difference: the spatial world, in contrast to the temporal world, is not riven, for Hardy, with feelings of dislocation, displacement and alienation. People, artefacts, places, strangers and friends, known and unknown, seem to frequent his imaginative life -- just as they enter his texts unannounced -- as everyday, idle presences. Those who mediate between worlds probable and possible, the obsolete past and a wished-for-futurity, with what 'might have been', what 'would have been', doggedly and very matter-of-factly intervene. They are not always consonant with the text, and they invariably displace the primary narrator, but they carry no nostalgia. As presences, they are endowed with no force from the past, no heartbeat of home, no memory of the ancestral village, no dream of the Golden Age, no longed-for green-and-pleasant land -- Old England. [3]

Yet, in this lovingly constructed world of the heartland, the country of origins, the natal homeland, Hardy's primary narrator does fall, as we have seen, out of place. And, in a manner of speaking, this seems appropriate to his expressed endeavour. There are several approaches one could make here: that narratorial self-displacement is stylistically appropriate in terms of pure poesis, in the sense that if verse had to give way to prose (an onus, an unwanted break, as Hardy experienced it), then why not apply a prosaic kind of *caesura*? Why not make a break with the very thing that he is now bound to relate -- Wessex, the lost past, etc? Another approach would be to regard this narratorial position as appropriate in psychological terms of creating, generating text, of 'mothering' the text. Should he, must he, can he let go (expel) the thing bound to be born in him? Less conjecturally, in terms of endeavour, this kind of narratorial vanishing is particularly appropriate to Hardy's sense of irony, in this case his ironic sense of the paradox that lies at the centre of writing-the-past -- as implied in his wished intent. He wished, he said, to preserve 'a fairly true record of a vanishing life.' [4] Not, that is, a 'true record' of the past, but rather of the past's passing -- the 'vanishing life' . [5] This much, then, Hardy's narrator can acknowledge, while also acknowledging (within the dramatic text) the necessary fact of vanishing witnesses, notably the vanishing primary narrator given to tracing fleeting impressions of the 'vanishing life' and its fast disappearing origins in the maternal abode.

Hardy's hold on the past then, his desire to preserve a 'fairly true record of a vanishing life', comes far closer, in its structural forms of settlement/unsettlement or repossession/dispossession, to the idea of 'nostos', as opposed to nostalgia. 'Nostos' has less of the anguish, less of the homesickness, and more of the instinctual drive, the unconscious force, simply to return 'home'. Hence 'Wessex', and what Hardy called his partly-real, partly dream-country. Hence his creation of an abode for a host of presences rooted as much in the ancestral village as in his own visionary reconstruction of a physical, geographical, contemporary world of which he himself is an indweller. He dreams a world in which to house the self, or the selves that presently haunt him, frequent him, displace, replace or, quite simply, place him. In creating a dwelling place, a homeland, a natural world embosomed, as he might say, by Mother Nature, Hardy makes the imaginative return to his birthplace *realisable*. [6] He doesn't exactly carve his name on every tree, but he does place his imprint on every barrow and hill, every woodland and field. He makes maps of Wessex. He superimposes fictitious names over the actual -- just as he returns imaginary characters, again and again, to his own birthplace: Bathsheba to her uncle's home in Weatherbury -- where he had uncles; Clym to his maternal home on Egdon -- a stone's throw from his own mother's home; the Henchards to Casterbridge, where Hardy himself became not mayor but magistrate; Angel Clare to the Vale of the Great Dairies where he too, had loved and lost -- and much more besides.

* * *

Hardy, then, moves beyond nostalgia to vivify something more closely resembling psychological journeys of recovery and loss; journeys of accommodation and, in certain of the earlier novels, journeys of completion -- 'completion' in the sense of rejoining the circle at the point of disjuncture. He had left the family circle at the point of becoming a professional writer; becoming a professional writer, he rewrites the family circle and peoples it with his own kind.

Psychoanalytic theory proposes that certain literary or figurative constructs reflect certain authorial levels of psychic assimilation of, say, desire, deprivation or loss. Similarly, fragments of the authorial self, or past selves, also exist, in some assimilated form or other within the fictional construct. In Hardy, from the time of his creation of Wessex, beginning around the mid 1870s, the world is peopled with rootless young characters in search of a place of settlement -- physically searching, emotionally searching, spiritually searching. The temporal settings of his novels, the 'Novels of Character and Environment' in particular, invariably revert to the mid-century, from the 1840s to the late 1860s. Thus, in terms of historical time he returns to the world into which he was born, [7] to the homeland of his youth centered around the birthplace he customarily spoke of as 'my mother's home'. [8] For the first thirty-three years of his life this had been his whole world. For the last fifty it would be his entire visionary universe.

Reaching now deeper into this world, into its significance as 'maternal abode', into its larger dimensions of figurative dislocation and displacement, I want to move from the narrator's 'vanishing' role to that of the nurturing (or otherwise) physical world of nature. The implications of this topic are vast but there are paradigms even in the small. One aspect of the small is the manner in which certain literary configurations shape the physical world of Mother Nature as a body-construct -- as the embodiment, say, of birthing, nurturing, fragmentation, loss and death. These figurations, in terms of the centrality of the nostos motif, aptly illustrate the notion of an embodied (maternal) homeland: originally, in the earlier novels, the embodiment of a unified world, ultimately the embodiment of disintegration.

With the focus placed more intently upon 'mothering the text' and processes of expulsion, that equally important part of the Wessex construct which evokes refreshing, sensual, vibrant, fertile landscapes has, for the moment, to be set aside. Hardy's world may be monolithic but it is not monomorphic. If we are looking then at a world of nature no longer offering safe havens, welcoming abodes, places of solace and repose, a world in which nurturing has been lost and in which the young rarely thrive, the line of disjuncture and loss is best perceived chronologically. As the Wessex novels proceed, the psychological line from Mother Nature as secure and benign, in Hardy's first novel, *Under the Greenwood Tree*, to 'Nature's treachery' in his last, *Jude*, pulls sharply at a sense of broken links, torn connections and lost origins. By the time we come to *Jude*,

'Nature's treachery' no longer whimpers but shrieks with infantile rage. The fury at nature's cruel laws is also the fury of the impotent self which cannot break with its own self-image as victim, as a thing untimely born -- or as Hardy felt about both his principals and himself, born prematurely, out of due time. Both his central characters in *Jude* experience themselves in this way, man and woman alike.

Here too, by a significant displacement of Mother Nature on to a man-made construct -- the home of the collegiate body -- literally, physically crumbling before the young Jude's yearning eyes, the desired object in the approval-seeking, acceptability struggle is the Christminster 'Alma Mater' of his fantasies and dreams. In this, as in the pursuit of the lost beloved, as in the quest for a desired object which remains unattainable, Jude's unrequited attachment fuels a frustration that continually feeds on the thing that starves it. Dreaming the 'Alma Mater' to be his emotional and spiritual home, his nurturing 'mother' 'well-pleased' with her beloved son, his ancestral dwelling even -- the abode of his literary fathers -- Jude dreams a kind of divine *family*, a phantasy family. And, just as the victim-self sees itself, in pathos, as heroic, so here the orphaned Jude becomes pathetically attached to chimeras, heroically abandoned. Hardy reinforces this motif with Jude's loss of Sue, the woman-beloved who exists for him at a complex psychological level as part-dream ('angel', 'star', 'ethereal'), and part-real. The 'real' woman casts him off; the 'dream' fuses with his own consciousness and becomes the spectral image in which he sees his own (victim) likeness. Sue is not only his dream-woman, his guiding light, his cherished friend, the mother of his children, she is also the only kinswoman he possesses, and certainly the only woman who so approximates the lost, young mother of infancy that he can run to her 'under the influence of a childlike yearning for the one being in the world to whom it seemed possible to fly'. [9]

In this harsh world of Hardy's last novel, in which two motherless cousins find but cannot keep love and kinship, the nostos theme has hollowed out to become literally and figuratively a journey out of origins into an unsafe world, a journey to the very edge of the Wessex homeland, a journey through a series of lost abodes to ultimate expulsion from the very pulse of life itself. For the two cousins there is a shared past and several last visits to their last living relative -- a dying aunt whose death unites them; for Arabella there are several last returns to Wessex in which she finally manages to cast off her motherhood. Significantly, the desired (Christminster) abode, with all its 'mothering' spaces in which to learn and make new discoveries, in which to grow and mature in protected safety, has become distorted, as in dream mechanisms, into something disturbingly familiar yet horrifyingly strange. Seemingly nurturing, it turns out to be actually annihilating; potentially approving, it turns out to be ultimately rejecting; believed to be protectively maternal, it turns out to be harshly, severely paternal -- or rather, co-extensively patriarchal. Correspondingly, Jude's own son, as if shaped in some grotesque form of Christminster's (the longed-for-home) harsh severity combined with the motherless orphan's psychic suffering, abandons life altogether while claiming his father's futurity -- the little babies he had created with his beloved Sue.

This kin-hungry world is a long way from Hardy's world in *Under the Greenwood Tree*, of 1871, published some twenty years earlier. Here we have family love and kinship in abundance. This gentle, humorous tale is told primarily through the eyes of the young Dick Dewy who, as his name suggests, possesses a kind of dewy-eyed innocence aptly matched to the story's simple scenes of congenial family gatherings, all of them lovingly detailed by Hardy.

However, the world of *Under the Greenwood Tree* is not, strictly speaking, the world of Wessex. It is not until Hardy has married and left the maternal home for good -- that is, the Bockhampton home from which many *Under the Greenwood Tree* scenes are taken -- that Wessex begins to take shape; although it is true to say that at the point of embarking on marriage in 1874 he does give intimations of what is to come, in *Far from the Madding Crowd*, by changing the names of a few much-loved Dorset hamlets, hills, valleys and towns, and by speaking of the region as 'Wessex' for the very first time. [10] However, no sooner has he begun to dream up this world than he departs, in *The Hand of Ethelberta*, in 1876, for the city. In open defiance of editors and critics clamouring for yet more 'Wessex' he had, he said, to prove that his interests ranged beyond cows and sheep.

As it happened, he proved this point far more effectively by subsequently returning to, and bringing fully into being the country which, in true Homeric style, could be fashioned to the most complex of psychological landscapes to reflect a whole host of human experiences and social conditions. For our purposes, this becomes the condition of uprooting and severance from family, home and mother. And it is with his next novel, the purposefully artistic *The Return of the Native*, in 1878, that this theme, interwoven with the now full-bodied Wessex construct, becomes firmly established. Moreover, Clym Yeobright's return to the maternal home signifies a critical turning point for Hardy: henceforth, there is no homecoming in the Wessex world which does not herald a tragic loss of love.

Before taking a closer look at *The Return of the Native*, I would like to touch, very briefly, on the general thematic progression of disjuncture and loss as it curves away from its starting point with the pastoral-idyll in *Under the Greenwood Tree*. With Hardy's next novel, *A Pair of Blue Eyes*, in 1873, there are prefatory glimpses of this lost, broken world, most notably in the natural-world setting which here becomes geographically marginalised. Removed from the Dorset birthplace and edging off into the furthest reaches of Wessex (as it will shortly become), the central location of this novel is an imaginative recreation of Emma Lavinia's home-country in Cornwall. Hardy was courting her at the time. Possibly, the lack of a unified setting in this novel arises from its having been written in different locations: the first instalment in London, the second in Cornwall, the next at home in Bockhampton, and so on. Howsoever this disunity arises, what the stable world of *Under the Greenwood Tree* possesses, the world of *A Pair of Blue Eyes* does not. Not only is there no unified setting but also no secure place of settlement and no satisfactory ascendancy of youth over age as in the preceding novel (the 'boy' Stephen mutely rivals but does not supersede his fatherly mentor, Henry Knight).[11] In fact, this is a world to leave, a world of perpetual departures, a veritable saga of broken journeys. From Elfride's attempt to flee her father by eloping to London, to Knight's premature return from his travels abroad to claim her as bride, to Stephen's voyage overseas to improve his prospects as her potential husband, down to the final journey when all three accidentally come together on the corpse-bearing train to the West Country, each 'return' in this novel involves some kind of break or loss. Each time there are severed connections, lost hopes and broken dreams. In this respect, despite the lack of a coherent topography or unified setting, *A Pair of Blue Eyes* goes some way towards implicating the voyager in a fruitless voyage home -- a theme shortly to become central to the Wessex *telos*.

As the novels proceed, and for those principals who return home to no immediate threat or loss, prefigurations of dislocation and disintegration in the natural world abound to such an extent that we rapidly lose sight of it as the regenerative world of Mother Nature. This manner of integrating the *broken* or *lost* object into the psychological landscape (the embodying construct), whether in fiction or fantasy formation, brings us back to the idea of the dream mechanism which fashions a loved face or place so distorted as to be beyond all recognition. If, according to psychoanalytic theory the dream mechanism, by this means, prepares us for separation and loss, this is certainly true of the literary construct. Readers of Hardy's later novel, *The Woodlanders* (1887), for example, have no difficulty in discerning that the world to which Grace Melbury returns as a woman (having left a young girl), is a world in which the blighted growth on the outside mirrors the condition of young human lives on the inside. We have, in the natural world, manifest correspondences to the world of the family which, here, fails to provide for the needs of its young. At the very outset, a promising young life returns home -- to where, incidentally, the birth-mother is lost -- and on the very first day of her return the sun itself almost fails to rise:

> presently the bleared white visage of a sunless winter day emerged like a dead-born child. (54)

Here, too, the life force of nature, unlike that in *Under the Greenwood Tree*, warps and distorts the growth of young trees:

> The leaf was deformed, the curve was crippled, the taper was interrupted; the lichen ate the vigour of the stalk, and the ivy slowly strangled to death the promising sapling. (83)

And here, too, there are disfiguring wounds:

> Sometimes a bough...was swayed so low as to smite the roof in the manner of a gigantic hand smiting the mouth of an adversary, to be followed by a trickle of rain, as blood from the wound. (335)

Or there is grotesque distortion and dismemberment of Mother Nature's bodily parts:

On older trees...huge lobes of fungi grew like lungs. (83)

Above stretched an old beech, with vast arm-pits, and great pocket-holes in its sides....Dead boughs were scattered about. (338)

Beneath them were the rotting stumps of those...vanquished long ago, rising from their mossy setting like black teeth from green gums. (339)

As we might expect from this grotesque distortion of a woodland world that in *Under the Greenwood Tree* had epitomized family unity, community intimacy and mother-love, this is no tale of past joys relived or youthful loves fulfilled. Instead, there are repeated acts of exclusion and expulsion, and all of them generated from within a community no larger than a small extended family: a family linked by kith and kin but completely fragmented into disparate parts -- dismembered as a body, and divested, as a generation, of birth-mothers and young children, of whom there are none.

In just over a decade, then, the benign Mother Nature of *Under the Greenwood Tree* undergoes a radical transformation to become noticeably more malign by the time Hardy comes to *The Woodlanders* (both internal settings, incidentally, are recreated from the woodland region flanking Hardy's birthplace). Gone is the woodland embodiment of safe enclosure and security (just as Hardy's own home stood solitary, secure and deep among dense woodland trees), and gone are the close-knit families staunchly buttressed against the outside world to the very last where we conclude with a wedding party and celebrations of union and regeneration.[12]

Such celebrations are not characteristic of Hardy. On the contrary, most Wessex weddings are dire. Nor did Hardy's own wedding celebration, during the serialisation of *Far from the Madding Crowd*, in 1874, in any way resemble a *Greenwood Tree* affair. But then *Greenwood* days were over. Hardy had made his last return to live at the Bockhampton cottage of his childhood. *Far from the Madding Crowd* would be the last of his novels to be written in his mother's home. And this would be the last time he would have the 'stimulus of his mother's companionship'. [13] Thus it is with heartfelt tenderness that he writes of being able to go home to where the nightingales sing in the garden -- a tenderness he had once expressed with all the vehemence of a young Clym Yeobright, when he had avowed, 'I will stay here till I die'.[14]

Four years later (after the publication of *Far from the Madding Crowd*, Hardy makes a conscious move back into the past: *The Return of the Native* is set in

41

the midcentury of his own boyhood. Here, in the seclusion of *his* mother's house -- all the more secluded for her recent death -- Clym's anguished cry is that he 'cannot die'. He cannot escape his life, he cannot reverse it. He cannot annihilate the tragedy of his marriage, of Eustacia's death, of the estrangement between mother and son, the rupture of families, the agonising sense that he, the beloved son, had cast off his own mother and that she had gone to her death believing herself outcast by him.

It is I who ought to have drowned myself...But I cannot die. Those who ought to have lived lie dead; and here am I alive! (447)

He cannot die, but rather sees himself caught in some kind of timeless emptiness, condemned to live out the horror of his existence, as he describes it. Feeling himself to be a veritable 'corpse of a lover' (465), with the memory of his mother as a 'sublime saint whose radiance even his tenderness for Eustacia could not obscure' (480), he cries out at the last:

O, my mother, my mother! would to God that I could live my life again, and endure for you what you endured for me! (480)

Clym *had* in fact reversed his life. He had returned, in the first instance, to re-occupy the maternal home, called Bloom's End -- itself an interesting naming, suggesting both the end of a youthful springtime and an ageing mother's loss of girlish 'bloom'. Yet, even at this original point of return Clym appears strangely like a wraith, a spectral self, materialising less as a physical flesh-and-blood presence than a being created purely out of utterance.

In the first place, he emerges, dim and indistinct, from atmospheric gloom: just as the 'dead-born' sun appears as a corpse on the horizon upon Grace's return to her birthplace, so with Clym's return at nightfall the sun is dying. Compounding the association between nostos and death, between the desire to return to the place of origins and being cast out of it, Hardy puts out the sun -- the embodiment of light and nurture, of life itself. Clym, then, puts his life into reverse in darkness. [15] He had left home to go out into the world, had journeyed to the city of light (Paris), had then repudiated the world in favour of his birthplace which upon his immediate return presents to him a face not only 'chilly' but also 'dark and lonely' (135). Furthermore, just as his murky advent is enshrouded by atmospheric obscurity -- as the gazing Eustacia perceives the scene, straining her eyes towards the maternal home -- so he is now seen as a disembodied form in line with his mother and cousin as, through the sombre darkness,

their heads became visible against the sky (135)

And no sooner has he half-emerged, wraith-like, not entirely whole, than he utters himself in a voice which dies upon the ear. Barely audible, he is identified as a 'masculine voice', one of three which 'passed on, and decayed and died upon her ear' (136).

Later, of course, Eustacia will become the lonely watcher of Clym's days as he toils on the heath with failing eyes, with a *vision* that will decay and die. However, for the moment he is but a dying voice; and it is not simply that he materialises out of utterance, as a construct of language somewhat indistinctly inscribed upon the natural world -- almost, one might say, the ghosted presence of a man -- but that this necessarily establishes him as an *idea*, emphatically so in Eustacia's mind. At the same time, Clym's own utterance of the natal world to which he is returning inscribes upon it configurations of the body. He speaks; Eustacia listens:

Sometimes this throat uttered Yes, sometimes it uttered No; sometimes it made inquiries about a timeworn denizen of the place. Once it surprised her notions by remarking upon the friendliness and geniality written in the faces of the hills around . (136)

It is worth noticing, at this point, that for this returning native the natal world exists, quite plainly, as a construct of language, and that configurations of the body, as inscribed upon and within objects in the natural world, construct their own logocentric universe (for Hardy, concentric: a world within a world within a world).

Clym's first incarnation as a fully visible physical body occupying a fully visible physical space occurs at the Bloom's End homecoming party -- that is, within the body of his mother's house. Yet even here, even on the inside of the maternal abode, he emerges as perishable tissue, his body wasted by thought. Correspondingly, conversations among the rustics turn upon coffins: analogically, upon the housing of the wasted body, upon the burial site for perishable tissue at the final homecoming.

If we return to the body-construct of the natural world, we now see the fittingness of Hardy's representation of Egdon, not only as birthplace/birthing place but also as a labyrinthine passage through darkness, through what Hardy calls the Egdon Hades. If Wessex itself embodies, in manifold proportions, a reconstructed homeland, then Egdon plausibly exemplifies -- as part of the projected form -- the monolithic body of the past out of which humanity is born and can never return. By extension, this exemplar reiterates the desire to hold on to the past, to conserve original attachments -- the 'nostos' of the returning native -- which begins and ends in modes of incompletion, in remembering and forgetting, in fragments of consciousness, in imagination and dreams. In this respect, Egdon, manifesting the irrecoverable territory of the past, serves aptly as a figuration of the past's indeterminacy, its fragmented elements, its odd, half-forgotten forms.

First there is the memorable opening scene. A slightly disturbing fragmentation of forms is emphasised by the way bodies appear and disappear, only partially visible in the darkness. Bits are pieced together but there is no wholeness. In addition there is the curious womb-like 'birthing' of the scene: it is twilight at first; there is a whitish-brownish dimness overall; the heaven is spread with a pallid screen; the distant rims of the world seem almost visible. There is breathing, an exhaling darkness. There is waiting and listening, a sense of 'midnight dreams of flight and disaster'. And as the fragmented bits and pieces gradually take shape, so out of the darkness three women emerge, each in indeterminate stages of remoteness, alienation or rejection.[16]

Upon Clym's return home he is to lose each of these women in turn. First he loses Thomasin (in marriage to Wildeve) from the maternal home: the woman he had loved as dearly as he would have loved a sister.[17] Then, he loses his mother: the woman with whom he had shared such deep affinities that it was as if 'their discourses were...carried on between the right and left hands of the same body' (222). And, finally, he loses Eustacia: the woman he had chosen to love, to 'fight for, support, help, be maligned for' (245).

Significantly, although the intimacy of these relationships is seen clearly by the narrator -- just as pre-existing conditions are seen to be inscribed upon Clym's own face, and just as Clym himself sees geniality 'written in the faces of the hills around' -- very little family intimacy is seen clearly by the reader. Affinities are spoken of but rarely made visible. There are glimpses, fragments merely. It is as if, at times, Hardy's primary narrator has indeed vanished from that 'vanishing life' -- or that the very record he would preserve has not survived the years. In accentuation of this 'vanishing life', the central characters not only continue to appear as half-lit fragments -- a hand, a profile, a disembodied voice, a figure glimpsed at a window, a fire-lit face -- but persistently miss their way on the heath at night. The inference is that they have forgotten or lost the signs that should be completely familiar to them, as natives. And were it not enough that they repeatedly lose themselves they also repeatedly mistake one another, in the darkness, for someone else.

The Egdon paradigm functions, then, as the irretrievable past, not only symbolically, in its fragmented, half-glimpsed people and places, and not only historically, in its age-old burial grounds and Roman artefacts, but also notationally, in its narrative gaps and silences. And as a paradigm it represents one of Hardy's most shattered psychological landscapes. Topographically, it has unified form. But at its epicentre it is, as Hardy says, a 'waste'. Here Clym will waste his days, his eyes will waste, his relationships will waste, his two beloved women will waste. And if the dramatic force of his nightmarish journey through loss of youth, loss of home, loss of mother, is anywhere inscribed at all, it is inscribed upon this waste.

As the breach widens, for example, between mother and son -- she tormented by the idea that he is wasting his life (226) -- he leaves home in turmoil. Instantly, lacerations appear in the landscape (247). Then, as the distressed mother treks across the heath to recover her lost son, instantly the earth begins to crack (324). Then, as she loses herself in trying to find him so the sky turns an unnatural metallic violet (325). Then, as she perceives (but fails to recognise) him as a distant figure toiling half-blind on the heath, so the very trees themselves turn 'blasted' (327).

The Egdon 'waste', at each and every point, mirrors that incompletion in Nature which is Clym's own psychological condition. This is, at once, his overwrought anxiety to repossess original attachments; his desire to 'complete' himself by replacing his male progenitor (father/author) in his mother's house; and his urge to re-enter the maternal abode from which separation is unendurable yet whose gap he cannot close. [18] The self's incompletion is mirrored in the way in which all bodies are seen as fragmented, in the way people meet by night and are thus identified only as shadowy, half-lit disconnected bits and pieces, eternally getting lost in a world of lost abodes. All of this intensifies the underlying motif of abandonment in this tale of lost-and-found connections, found-and-lost origins, in this most haunting of all Hardy's twilight worlds through which the soul voyages half-blind, half-seen, half-heard and never more than half-complete.

After the publication of *The Return of the Native*, Hardy makes one or two forays beyond Wessex, notably in *The Trumpet-Major* (1880) and *The Laodicean* (1881), and returns for good and all (physically, in the mid-eighteen-eighties to move to Max Gate at Dorchester), with the publication of *The Mayor of Casterbridge* in 1886. Between the years 1871 and 1897 he published fourteen novels, most of which express, in varying degrees of complexity and subtlety, the forms and cyclical patterns of classical pastoral elegy -- of scenarios spatially continuous with life. And, as his novels proceed, pursuing in turn the gradual dissolution of the pastoral, so the symbolic forms and configurations embodying the dying spirit of nature less frequently, less emphatically modulate into the renewal, rebirth, resurrection and regeneration characteristic of the pastoral genre: that after death and burial, grief and mourning, there comes release: release from the darkness into the light, from despair into hope, from resignation into the promise of renewed life in Nature. By the time we come to *Jude*, there is no cycle of renewal, no hint of rebirth, no whisper of resurrection, not the smallest hope of 'return'. And, aside from Hardy's narrator, nobody mourns. There is even a dearth of visitants. Where are they now, those presences who 'might have seen' another world, who might have cast out Hardy's primary narrator from the tragic world-in-view, if only for momentary relief from it?

Jude, like his author, had not wanted to grow up to be a man. Of all projections of despair, of loss of childhood, of separation from home and the maternal abode, these projections in *Jude the Obscure* are Hardy's most painful and unresolved. For, after all, the impoverished, love-starved orphan with no safe refuge in the world should have nothing much to lose by growing up. Except his life.

The sublime indifference of all things in Jude's hour of need leaves him with one last, lonely cry: to be at peace. To identify with the susceptibility seems paramount in Hardy. The lost boy-self mourned and laid to rest so compassionately by the 'mothering' text in *Jude*, puts finally to rest the Wessex homeland and the restless, uprooted souls roaming therein. Perhaps, then, to be placed in momentary relation to that 'vanishing life' of past years was, after all, one way of going home -- one way of being, at last, at peace.

NOTES

1   These lines are taken from 'Wessex Heights', which Hardy finished writing in December 1896. Martin Seymour-Smith, who notes that 'ghosts were so natural' in Hardy's outlook, speaks of a 'holographic blur' coming into focus 'when the entire poem has been registered in the mind'. See *Hardy*, Martin Seymour-Smith (Bloomsbury Publishing Ltd., London, 1994) pp. 582-3. I think Hardy would have enjoyed the whole concept of holography -- or any form of virtual imaging.

2   See also U.C. Knoepflmacher, 'Hardy's Ruins: Female Spaces and Male Designs', in *The Sense of Sex: Feminist Perspectives on Hardy*, edited by Margaret R. Higgonet (University of Illinois Press, Urbana & Chicago, 1993), pp. 107-131.

Knoepflmacher points to Hardy's poem, 'Domicilium', written between the ages of 17 and 20, as a site of 'revisitation' in which the poet recovers the grandmother's voice as a 'memory-trace' -- a route to the past -- she, herself, remaining 'a figuration of desire that must adapt itself, however reluctantly, to "change"'. Knoepflmacher also draws comparisons between Hardy's reliance on a 'dead female agent' and Wordsworth's use of 'feminine space' with its indirect association with dream memories of an original maternal envelope. Of all the keen points made in Knoepflmacher's essay I find the following particularly apt:

> The mother Hardy associates with his own creativity becomes a focal point for the tug-of-war between a childlike desire for sustained fusion and an adult insistence on the necessity for detachment.

3   The notalgic yearning for a lost past in Matthew Arnold's poem, 'The Scholar Gypsy', which cries out for this 'long unhappy dream' to end (as if there will be, should be, an awakening), is not a yearning we find in Hardy.

4 Thomas Hardy, 'General Preface to the Wessex Edition of 1912', October 1911.

5 In terms of writing-the-past in a slightly different context, and in arguing against John Bayley's perception of *The Trumpet -Major* as an historical novel pure and simple -- specifically, Bayley's failure to recognise Hardy's resistance to genre -- Richard Nemesvari touches on the issue of Hardy's purposeful invocation of 'a kind of temporal disjunction' and of his problematising of historical 'reality'.

In its original form the novel's juxtaposition of fiction and history created a subdued kind of tension....and the availability of historical 'reality' becomes much more problematic [when this] juxtaposition becomes overt....The reader of *The Trumpet Major* is therefore faced with a kind of temporal disjunction, for Hardy purposefully invokes the past while resolutely avoiding history...
      Richard Nemesvari, 'The Anti-Comedy of *The Trumpet -Major*',
      The Victorian Newsletter, Spring 1990, No. 77, pp. 8-13.

6 In this instance with Cybele-the-Many-Breasted in mind.

7 Hardy was born in Bockhampton, Dorset, in 1840.

8 See also Michael Millgate, *Thomas Hardy: a Biography* (Oxford, Melbourne: Oxford University Press, 1982) p. 21.

9 *Jude the Obscure*, Norton Critical Edition, edited by Norman Page, 1978, p. 100.

10 Many of these were altered by Hardy later to cohere with the Wessex construct.

11 Hardy's paternal great-grandfather married into a family named 'Knight'.

12 If we regard *Under the Greenwood Tree* purely in the light of its stability, its coherent integration of time and place, there might be an interesting case to be made for self-affirmation on Hardy's part. Putting his father's world 'out' so to speak, which was in autobiographical terms, with the disbanding of the church choir, the world of his grandfather also, and replacing it with a new order (with the introduction of a new *instrument*, the church organ), the son effectively establishes a voice separate and distinct from that of his father or forefathers. Figuratively speaking the ancient male chorus dies and the literary son is born. The important point of contrast is, however, that at this stage the literary son is self-confidently 'at home' in a psychological landscape to which he will later return with increasing manifestations of dislocation.

13 Cited by Michael Millgate, *op cit.*, p. 153.

14 Millgate, *op cit.*, p. 115.

15 This later becomes literally the case, as he begins to lose his sight.

16 By coincidence or unconscious design there had also been three much-loved women, a mother and two sisters, in the Bockhampton family home.

17 In Hardy's first conception of things Thomasin was Clym's sister. Perhaps here, Hardy has in mind his own mother's wish that the Hardy children should all live together for the rest of their lives, just as Mrs. Yeobright wishes for her beloved, daughterly Thomasin to marry her son, Clym (which as cousin Thomasin could do if as sister she could not). Michael Millgate (*op cit.*, p. 21) says of Hardy's mother that,

> She wanted them never to marry but to live together in pairs, a son and a daughter, and thus maintain throughout life the unity and interdependence of their childhood.

18 'Womb' suggests itself, but it is, I think, too hackneyed a term and too simplistic a concept.

The 'Modernity' of Hardy's
Jude the Obscure

Robert Schweik

The range and variety of Hardy's influence on modern novelists has by now been more than amply demonstrated, [1] and the connection of some aspects of his *Jude the Obscure* to subsequent developments in the novel has long been acknowledged: it has become a commonplace to say, for example, that Hardy strongly influenced the treatment of human sexuality in the modern novel from D.H. Lawrence onward. As Ian Gregor put it, 'where *Jude* ends *The Rainbow* begins'. [2]

But if the influence of Hardy's *Jude* on the history of the novel is unquestionable, its 'modernity' has been sharply disputed. One reason for the dispute lies in the way that claims for -- and denials of -- the 'modernity' of *Jude the Obscure* tend to be set forth. Irving Howe, for example, describes *Jude* in the following terms:

> *Jude the Obscure* is Hardy's most distinctly 'modern' work, for it rests upon a cluster of assumptions central to modernist literature: that in our time men wishing to be more than dumb clods must live in permanent doubt and intellectual crisis; that for such men, to whom traditional beliefs are no longer available, life has become inherently problematic ... and that courage, if it is to be found at all, consists in readiness to accept pain while refusing the comforts of certainty. [3]

Such sweeping claims for the 'modernity' of *Jude* have led to equally sharp denials, perhaps the most categorical of which is that by C.H. Salter:

> [Hardy] uses the word *modern* vaguely and applies it to much that is not really modern or only trivially so, and sometimes as a term of reproach. He expresses a pessimism not produced by modern causes, but timeless and congenital .... Hardy's idea of tragedy is simple and medieval. [4]

In disagreements of this kind, both sides tend to make sweeping assumptions that 'modernity' is reducible to some central ideological stance which a work of art might or might not reflect. But, particularly in the nineteenth and twentieth centuries, works of high art exhibit exceptional diversity of form and matter -- an array of more or less distinct, often obscurely related, widely varying, and frequently conflicting attitudes and techniques -- and an equal diversity of relationships to their cultural context. Seeking some centre in that diversity is an exercise in futile reductivity, and all but useless in attempting to define the 'modernity' of a work of art like *Jude* -- especially given the conclusions of recent studies about its profound ambiguities. [5]

Rather, in art history -- and particularly for the nineteenth and twentieth centuries -- it is far wiser to proceed on the assumption that whatever may be said to constitute the 'modernity' of a given work of art must inevitably be the product of selective retrospection: the identification of some of its features as 'modern' because, from the vantage point of a later time, they can be seen to have been at the leading edge of one or another notable change beginning to take place in the arts. Describing the way any given work of art combines such features can be a useful way of identifying its peculiar kind of 'modernity'. It is in this way that I want to consider the 'modernity' of *Jude the Obscure*. The claim I make here is that in *Jude* -- apart from the ways in which Hardy rendered his characters' sexuality -- it is possible to identify three techniques remarkably similar to those beginning to be adopted by other artists in different countries and in different media at almost exactly the same time, and that, in this respect, *Jude the Obscure* was at the forefront of three important developments in the history of Western art -- and 'modern' in that way. The changes I am concerned with are these:

1. the growing practice of ending works of art in ways that deny the audience a sense of resolution and closure,

2. the emergence of the kinds of unusual distortion and simplification characteristic of certain forms of expressionist art, and

3. the beginnings of a practice of mixing sharply conflicting artistic modes in a single art work.

Subsequently these strategies would be exploited in extreme forms in many works of art associated with 'modernism'.

Some of the ways *Jude* embodies these features have been partly described; [6] others have not, however, nor has their striking conjunction in the novel and their relationship to the emergence of parallel strategies in other art forms in the years 1893-4 been pointed out.

Techniques for Denying Readers a Sense of Final Resolution and Closure

A greater willingness to find new kinds of endings was one notable consequence of the growing rage for innovation in late nineteenth- and early twentieth-century art, and those innovations were put to an enormously wide range of artistic purposes. Among these was the use of a complex of devices for creating a more open-ended art work -- one which, in Robert Martin Adams' phrase, included 'a major unresolved conflict with the intent of displaying its unresolvedness'. [7] Devices to create that kind of 'openness' came to be employed with greater frequency and obviousness from the end of the century onward.

Some few signs of increasing willingness of novelists to exploit such endings began to appear after the middle of the nineteenth century in England and on the Continent. For example in both *Madame Bovary* (1857) and *L'Education Sentimentale* (1869), Flaubert gave the final words to a character who speaks simplistic banalities that leave the reader with no concluding authorial overview which might create a surer sense of resolution. Of the two endings Dickens wrote to *Great Expectations* (1861), the first would have denied readers the sense of resolution that comes from the conventional use of a marriage to suggest an achieved happiness. Hardy, too, claimed that in the composition of *The Return of the Native* he had intended to have a more 'open' ending -- again without a marriage -- but was discouraged from doing so by the conventions required by serial publication. [8]

From that time forward, however, the endings of Hardy's major fiction reveal a tentative movement toward the use of less resolved endings. A marked lack of resolution is notable in *The Woodlanders*, for example, though it is softened by Marty South's final apostrophe to Giles Winterborne. [9] Even at the conclusion of *Tess*, Hardy provided a very important suggestion of some possibility of a happier future for Angel Clare in the company of a 'spiritualized' Tess: her younger sister, Liza Lu. [10] It was only with *Jude* that Hardy finally created a narrative ending which not only left major issues emphatically unresolved but also suggested pointedly that the suffering and deprivation endured by one of its major characters would continue.

What is striking about *Jude* is both the multiplicity of techniques Hardy exploited in it to create that unresolved open-endedness, and also the way one of those techniques was paralleled by a similar development in music at almost exactly the same time.

To emphasize the lack of resolution in *Jude*, Hardy adopted at least three major devices. First, as Alan Friedman has noted, the counterpointed treatment of marriage and funeral at the end of the novel deprives both marriages of the traditional effect of closure these familiar endings usually have. Second, as Daniel Schwartz and Peter Casagrande have pointed out, *Jude the Obscure* has a 'cyclical' plot pattern and an 'iterative structure' of remarriages and returns of scenes and characters which helps create a sense of pointless getting nowhere.

51

David Sonstroem's diagram of the monotonously repeated back-and-forth pattern of Jude's movements in the novel suggests in still another way just how very repetitive its structure really is. [11]

But certainly the most powerful of the formal devices Hardy used to create the sense of unresolved open-endedness notable in *Jude* is the prolonged pattern of Jude's gradually diminishing aspirations, and the repeated checks on them which come in increasingly quick succession, and at progressively lower levels, in ten stages:

1. Jude first aspires to become a Bishop. (I, 1-9) [12]

2. Frustrated by Arabella's trick, he less confidently tries again; but, rejected by the college masters, he recognizes the collapse of his university hopes. (II, 1-7).

3. He then aspires to enter the church as a licentiate; but, baffled by Sue's marriage to Phillotson, he spends the night with Arabella, and experiences a weakening of his faith and his ambition for ecclesiastical life. (III, 1-10)

4. Jude nevertheless persists in his studies; but, when Sue flees to him, he finds his feelings for her inconsistent with his ecclesiastical ambitions, burns his books, and abandons his hope to be a clergyman. (IV, 1-3)

5. Jude next seeks fulfillment with Sue; but he is frustrated by her sexual reticence and her unwillingness to marry which brings upon them such social disapproval that they are driven to wandering from town to town. (IV, 5; V, 4-7)

6. After years of wandering, Jude aspires only to live peacefully in Christminster; but, returning there, he feels his humiliation more keenly and is faced with the catastrophe of his children's deaths and Sue's distraught reaction to it. (V, 8; VI, 3-7)

7. Sue's return to Phillotson reduces Jude to a bare hope for her possible return; but even this small aspiration is destroyed by her intransigence and by Jude's entrapment in a loveless marriage with Arabella. (VI, 3-7)

8. In the end Jude is reduced to seeking nothing more than his own death by exposing himself to the rain and cold; but even his suicide attempt is thwarted by a recovery that enables him to return to work. (VI, 8-10)

9. When his health finally does break down, Jude's last wish for water goes unheard, his barely whispered quotation of Job is mocked by the repeated 'Hurrah' of the Remembrance Day crowd, and his death itself becomes only a vexing inconvenience to Arabella as she goes about the business of attracting a new lover. (VI, 11)

10. In the final image of the novel, even Jude's remaining books -- the relics of his previous ambition -- seem 'to pale to a sickly cast' at the Remembrance Week noise, while the novel's last words emphasize that Sue's suffering will continue. (VI,11)

If we were to represent graphically this pattern of Jude's progressively declining aspirations and the repeated checks upon them, they would appear as a line with a succession of peaks representing his aspirations followed by a subsequent decline, the peaks and valleys becoming progressively lower and flatter, until reduced to scarcely more than a ripple -- but never quite terminating because even the finality of Jude's death is compromised by the prediction that Sue's pitiful sufferings will go on. [13]

The increasing employment of 'open' endings in the history of the novel after the publication of *Jude* has been extensively studied -- notably by Alan Fried-man, Beverly Gross, Frank Kermode, David H. Richter, and most searchingly, by Maria Torgovnick [14]. These studies make clear that when Hardy publish-ed *Jude* in 1895 he was at the leading edge of what would become a widespread use of unresolved endings in literature. Such endings began to be more com-monly used in the decades immediately following the publication of *Jude*; they show up in such disparate novels as Lawrence's *Sons and Lovers* (1913), Ford's *The Good Soldier* (1915), and Forster's *A Passage to India* (1924). And, in later fiction such devices appear with greater frequency and in more extreme forms -- often in major touchstones of 'modernist' literature. Faulkner's *Absalom, Absalom!* (1936) and some of Samuel Beckett's works -- to cite just two very different examples -- are notorious for the ways they deny audiences a sense of resolution.

So much did such endings become a staple of twentieth-century literature that they have achieved the status of having become themselves conventional; as Maria Torgovnick wryly observed, 'by the nineteen-sixties and nineteen-seventies, the "open" ending had become too trite and expected to have great imaginative force'. [15] In short, the multiple formal features Hardy exploited to create a sense of lack of resolution in *Jude* put that novel squarely at the beginning of a movement toward unresolved endings which would quickly emerge as one characteristic feature of much modern literature.

There are parallels in music to such literary narrative strategies, [16] and it is not surprising to find the emergence of similar devices in music beginning almost precisely at the time *Jude* was published. Note, for example, the remark-able structural similarity between Hardy's *Jude* and the conclusion of the final movement of Tchaikovsky's *Sixth Symphony* , premiered just two years earlier on October 28, 1893, at St. Petersburg. Tchaikovsky not only ended it with a slow movement -- something all but unheard of in the history of the symphony -- but devised a series of sweeping musical lines in which the melody seems to heave itself up, then collapse back down, then repeat that pattern at a lower pitch; instead of resolving into a well-defined conclusion, they grow darker in

colour, and finally die very gradually away in an extraordinarily long diminu-
endo to the *pppp* of Tchaikovsky's final notation.

That unusual final movement unsettled the audience at its premiere; struc-
turally it bears a striking resemblance to the pattern of successively diminished
aspirations and defeats which is one of the central formal features of Hardy's
novel. Moreover, Tchaikovsky's note on his *Sixth Symphony* emphasizes that he
had in mind a programme in which life is imaged as first impulsive passion and
confidence, followed by disappointments, collapse of hopes, and death [17] --
a programme that squares remarkably with Hardy's obvious intentions in *Jude*.
It is not at all surprising that some ten years later, after Hardy had heard the
Sixth Symphony, he would write that he detected the 'modern note of unrest' in
Tchaikovsky's music. [18]

And, as in the history of literature since Hardy's *Jude*, so in the history of
music, since the first performance of Tchaikovsky's *Sixth Symphony* in 1893, a
wide range of strategies which create a sense of lack of resolution emerged, and,
again, they were put to increasingly varied uses. Just three years after the first
performance of the *Sixth Symphony*, Richard Strauss ended his *Also Sprach
Zarathustra* (1896) in a torturously indecisive way by allowing a B major/C
major conflict of tonalities to go entirely unresolved. Gustav Mahler, to
mention yet another example, ended his *Ninth Symphony* (1910) with scattered
musical phrases that seemingly trail into nowhere; and, just one year later, Igor
Stravinsky chose to end his 1911 version of *Petrushka* by having the orchestra
fade to a whisper and end on an unresolved melodic dissonance -- a C natural
followed by an F sharp. In fact, within twenty years such endings became as
much a commonplace in music as in literature; today, discussion of the
circularity and sense of getting nowhere common in the works of such composers as Philip Glass and David Del Tredici and in the writings of John Barth,
Thomas Pynchon, and Donald Barthelme, has filtered down to the level of
the Sunday Supplement article. [19]

My first observation, then, is that in denying his readers a sense of resolution
in *Jude the Obscure*, Hardy was at the forefront in adopting a technique which,
in many variations, would figure prominently in subsequent developments not
only in literature but in music.

Expressionist Elements in Jude

A second feature notable in *Jude* puts that novel at the beginning of a very
different development in literature -- and one that played an important role in
the history of the visual arts as well. In some places in *Jude*, Hardy adopted a
style in which he attempted to intensify the expression of feeling and attitude
by exaggeration, simplification and distortion -- in short, by the use of devices
which are among the distinctive elements of certain kinds of 'expressionist' art.
What is striking about *Jude* is the relatively narrow range in which Hardy
employed those narrative strategies and the intensive use he made of them to

create a single character. Well-known notes by Hardy from the period 1886-1890 testify to his interest in such devices:

My art is to intensify the expression of things....

The 'simply natural' is interesting no longer. The much-decried, mad, late-Turner rendering is now necessary to create my interest.

Art is a disproportioning -- (i.e., distorting, throwing out of proportion) -- of realities, to show more clearly the features that matter in those realities... [20]

Hardy's emphasis on intensification and distortion to convey the artist's subjective sense of reality is consistent with the practices and theories of expressionist art whose precursors in literature and painting were emerging just at the time Hardy wrote *Jude*. Of course 'expressionism' took a wide variety of forms, but intense subjectivity, hyperbole, simplification and distortion to emphasize extreme, often pathological psychological states are some features often associated with it. In *Jude* such 'expressionist' features appear in places where characters exhibit exaggerated psychological states and the narrator's comments involve extreme distortions of reality -- for example, in Hardy's description of Jude's despair when he is confronted with the difficulties of learning Latin and Greek:

...he wished ... that he had never been born.

Somebody might have come along that way who would have asked him his trouble, and might have cheered him....But nobody did come, because nobody does; and under the crushing recognition of his gigantic error Jude continued to wish himself out of the world. (I-4)

Such extreme exaggerations of feeling and distortions of reality -- 'but nobody did come, because nobody does' -- constitute one major stylistic feature of *Jude*. They appear in such hyperboles as Mrs. Edlin's comment, 'Weddings be funerals 'a b'lieve nowadays', but, most importantly, Hardy used this mode to render Little Father Time almost entirely out of anti-realistic exaggerations. He is a walking hyperbole; the following quotations are entirely characteristic of the language in the novel -- both description and dialogue -- used to depict him:

He was Age masquerading as Juvenility....[H]is face took a back view over some great Atlantic of Time, and appeared not to care about what it saw. (V-3)

The boy seemed to have begun with the generals of life and never to have concerned himself with the particulars. (V-3)

'His face is like the tragic mask of Melpomene'. (V-4)

'The doctor says there are such boys springing up amongst us....He says it is the beginning of the universal wish not to live'. (VI-2)

'I should like the flowers very very much, if I didn't keep on thinking they'd be all withered in a few days!' (V-5)

'I ought not be born, ought I?' (VI-1)

The use of such techniques to convey an emotionally charged view of reality was emerging in literature, specifically in the plays of August Strindberg, just about the time Hardy produced *Jude*. As early as 1887, Strindberg's play *The Father* made a sharp departure from current realistic conventions; and by 1898, just three years after the publication of *Jude*, Strindberg had completed two parts of his *To Damascus* trilogy, the first fully expressionist literary work in which canons of realism are violated in favor of manipulating highly simplified characters expressive of extreme feeling. Typical features of Strindberg's expressionist mode are notable in the lines given to his character 'Stranger' in *To Damascus*:

....If I even knew why I was born -- why I should be standing here -- where to go -- what to do! Do you believe that we can be doomed already here on earth?

...when I thought I had found happiness, it was only a trap to lure me into a greater misery....Whenever the golden apple fell into my hand, it was either poisoned or rotten at the core.

...my fate is being ruled by two different forces, one giving me all that I ask for, the other standing beside me tainting the gift, so that when I receive it, it is so worthless that I don't want to touch it. [21]

Father Time would be entirely at home in such a play; even his nickname would be consistent with Strindberg's device of using general rather than specifically personal names.

Expressionist techniques such as Strindberg exploited in his dramas just at the time *Jude* was published were also appearing in Germany in the plays of Frank Wedekind, whose *Spring's Awakening* (1891) shocked audiences by its exploitation of grotesque caricature, its use of scenes with absurdist elements and, in the last act, its abandonment of realistic conventions by the introduction of that eerie character, The Man in the Mask, to express Wedekind's views. Subsequently the use of generalized characters and other devices pioneered by Strindberg and Wedekind appeared almost simultaneously in such disparate productions as Oskar Kokoschka's *Murder, Hope of Women* (1907), Wassily Kandinsky's *The Yellow Sound* (1909), Schoenberg and Poppenheim's *Expectation* (1909), and later in such literary works as Eugene O'Neill's *The Great God Brown* (1925) and Sean O'Casey's *The Silver Tassie* (1928). Characters that serve as metaphors for ideas and extremes of feeling, as Hardy's Father Time does, would subsequently appear prominently in 'modernist' literature: James Joyce, for example, used a variation on that technique to depict Bloom's innermost desires in the 'Circe' section of *Ulysses*, and, in extreme form it may be found in such works as Kafka's *The Transformation* , where the metaphor becomes embodied as realistically treated fact.

Hardy's use of such techniques in *Jude* just at the time when expressionism was emerging in the literature of Europe was paralleled by a similar development in painting. In December, 1893, just two years before *Jude* was published, Edvard Munch exhibited his proto-expressionist collection titled *The Frieze of Life* in Berlin. [22] There are images among those works which vividly replicate expressionist elements in *Jude*: Munch's painting titled *The Girl and Death*, for example, might serve as a visual rendering of Mrs. Edlin's observation 'Weddings be funerals 'a b'lieve nowadays', and his well-known *The Scream* could scarcely find a more fitting counterpart in the fiction of his day than in Hardy's Father Time. [23]

Furthermore, Munch's description of his paintings as 'nature transformed according to one's subjective disposition' and his expressed intention to paint not physical appearances but emotional reactions to them [24] -- these all accord with Hardy's views quoted earlier. Munch's use of deformed, hallucinatory images and his intensification of natural colour had an enormous impact on many artists who have subsequently been identified with 'expressionism': clearly he influenced the *Die Brücke* painters, especially Emil Nolde, and served as an immediate model for the later twentieth-century expressionists who formed the Berlin *Sezession* and others who followed them. [25]

In short, by exploiting distinctly expressionist elements in *Jude*, Hardy was once again at the beginning of a powerful movement towards one manifestation of 'modernism' in art -- one that cut across national boundaries and appeared in parallel ways in different mediums.

Employing Sharply Contrasting Artistic Modes

In 1887 Zola wrote to Strindberg criticising his play *The Father* for what today would be called its expressionist elements -- the 'schematic nature' of its characters, their 'lack of reality', the use of types rather than individuals and Strindberg's 'lack of concern for naturalistic plausibility'. [26] It certainly would not have occurred to Zola to consider injecting a character from a Strindberg play into one of his novels. Yet, that, in effect, is what Hardy did in *Jude the Obscure*. The expressionist devices Hardy used to render Father Time in *Jude* were very much like those employed by Strindberg -- and sharply at odds with the bulk of the novel.

As Michael Millgate has pointed out, Time is the sole exception to the other, more firmly realized characters in *Jude*, [27] and the styles Hardy adopted throughout the bulk of the novel were in the tradition of realistic fiction. [28] Such scenes as the fight that erupts at the meeting where Phillotson contests his dismissal (IV-6) had, as Hardy was aware, something of Fielding's comic realism [29], but in *Jude* this Fieldingesque manner blends into styles and techniques more characteristic of Flaubert and Zola. In Jude's deathbed scene, for example, Hardy sets Jude's dying words against the background of the cries of the Remembrance Week crowd -- a strategy reminiscent of Flaubert's device of having Rodolphe's seduction of Emma Bovary take place against the back-drop of speeches at an agricultural fair. And equally memorable are those scenes which strike us, as they struck Hardy's contemporaries, as Zolaesque: [30] the scene where Jude and Arabella take tea in an 'inn of an inferior class' (I,7) has elements reminiscent of *The Dram Shop*, for example, and the pig-killing (I,10) of *The Earth.* [31] In short, Father Time's appearance in *Jude the Obscure* is as if a character from Strindberg's *To Damascus* had somehow wandered into a novel of Fielding, Flaubert, Zola -- or Hardy.

At the time *Jude* was published, the beginnings of such mixing of sharply contrasting artistic modes were just appearing in Western art. One striking early example is Joris-Karl Huysmans' *En Rade* (1887) which so jarringly combined dream and reality that Zola wrote a letter to Huysmans complaining that the result was a 'confusion qui n'est pas de l'art'. [32] In the later work of Henrik Ibsen this mixing of sharply contrasting artistic modes took the form of con-joining the domestic realism of his earlier period with the symbolism notable in his plays from *The Wild Duck* (1884) onward, so that in *The Master Builder* (a play Hardy saw in 1893) [33] Ibsen's symbolism rubs shoulders with a realism as markedly different from it as Solness's references to a 'proper castle in the air' are to the 'real foundation' he proposes to build under it. [34]

This practice of mixing sharply contrasting artistic modes would subsequently become one of the most distinctive features of modernist art. One thinks of the quotations and allusions to literary and musical classics juxtaposed against gritty scenes of contemporary British life in *The Waste Land* (1922), and the similar collage-like mixing of sharply contrasting modes in Ezra Pound's *Cantos* (1917-1970). Virginia Woolf exploited another variation on the same strategy in *To the Lighthouse* (1927) by abruptly shifting from the minutely detailed and intensely personal interior monologues of the first and last sections of the novel to the impersonal, detached, and sweepingly general narrative style of the 'Time Passes' section. And, again, the device was pushed to its extreme limits in Joyce's *Ulysses* (1922), where shifts from one stylistic mode to another, sometimes within the space of a single chapter, occur with bewildering variety.

Conjoining sharply contrasting literary modes in one novel -- as Hardy combined elements of literary realism with those of literary expressionism in *Jude* -- also has a parallel in music: it is as if a composer were to have differnt parts of an orchestra playing in two dissonant musical keys in the same composition. And, in fact, at just the time Hardy was working on *Jude*, precisely that kind of development was taking place in music. Some time between 1892 and 1895 Charles Ives added an 'Interlude' to his *Variations on 'America'* in which he combined F major with A-flat major. [35] In the following years other composers began to exploit that same technique: Richard Strauss's modulation from G-minor to D-minor over a G flat major pedal chord in the love music of *A Hero's Life* (1898); Ravel's *Water Games* (1901) which juxtaposed C-major and F-major; Prokofiev's piano composition *Sarcasms* (1912-14) with B-flat minor in the left hand playing against F-sharp minor in the right. And, in the works of one modern composer, Darius Milhaud, the technique was pushed to the extreme of using three and four keys simultaneously. By 1920 the practice had already become so widespread that in the following decade it prompted a series of published analyses. [36]

Conclusion

If here we seem to be at a far remove from Hardy, my point is that, in his mixing of expressionistic and realistic modes in *Jude* in 1895, he was again at the forefront of a development which cut across artistic forms and national boundaries and led to major formal innovations characteristic of some of the touchstones of later twentieth-century art.

In her *Hardy and the Sister Arts*, Joan Grundy speculated about whether there were features in *Jude* which anticipated such later artistic developments as Cubism or Futurism and noted that 'the experience of modern life imaged at the start of the novel...certainly suggests a context similar to that out of which such art movements have sprung.' [37] I have attempted here to point out some of the ways *Jude* was indeed part of a context out of which a number of distinctive features of modernist art have emerged. Hardy's use of multiple formal devices which convey a sense of unresolved and problematic open-endedness; his adoption of an expressionist style in portions of the novel; and, even more, his mixing of sharply contrasting literary modes -- all these are striking instances of his early use of distinctive formal strategies which show up with growing frequency in modern literature and other artistic mediums. The increasingly pervasive use of those strategies in the arts from the publication of *Jude* onward makes clear that Hardy was working at the leading edge of some of the major artistic movements of his day, and by identifying these particular features it is possible to specify in a relatively precise way just how Hardy's *Jude the Obscure* may be said to have been in its time a 'modern' novel.

NOTES

1 See Peter J. Casagrande, *Hardy's Influence on the Modern Novel* (Totowa, New Jersey: Barnes & Noble Books, 1987).

2 Ian Gregor, *The Great Web: The Form of Hardy's Major Fiction* (Totowa, NJ: Rowman & Littlefield, 1987), p. 233.

3 Irving Howe, *Thomas Hardy* (New York: The Macmillan Company, 1967), p. 134.

4 C.H. Salter, *Good Little Thomas Hardy* (Totowa, NJ: Barnes & Noble Books, 1981), p. 26.

5 See, for example, Ramon Saldivar's 'Jude the Obscure: Reading and the Spirit of the Law', in Harold Bloom's *Thomas Hardy's Jude the Obscure* (New York: Chelsea House Publishers, 1987), pp. 103-118, and the summary points made by Gary Adelman, *Jude the Obscure: A Paradise of Despair* (New York: Twayne Publishers, 1992), pp. 29-30, 98, and 107.

6 In *Hardy and the Sister Arts* (London: Macmillan, 1979), p. 26, Joan Grundy briefly suggests a possible formal connection of *Jude* to Cubism, Futurism, and Vorticism, but does not pursue the matter further; also, in 'Some Surrealist Elements in Hardy's Prose and Verse', *Thomas Hardy Annual*, No. 3 (London: Macmillan, 1985), Rosemary Sumner has pointed to relationships of some aspects of Hardy's art -- though not of *Jude* -- to certain features of works of DeChirico, Ernst, Picasso, Magritte, and Duchamp.

7 Robert Martin Adams, *Strains of Discord: Studies in Literary Openness* (Ithaca, NY: Cornell University Press, 1958), p. 13.

8 See Carl J. Weber, 'Hardy's Grim Note in *The Return of the Native*', *Papers of the Bibliographical Society of America*, 36 (1942), 37-45. About how the present conclusion of *The Return of the Native* reinforces the doubts raised by the novel rather than resolves them, see Robert Schweik, 'Theme, Character and Perspective in Hardy's *The Return of the Native*', *Philological Quarterly*, 41 (1962) 757-767.

9 Robert Schweik, 'The Ethical Structure of Hardy's *The Woodlanders*', *Archiv fur das Studium der Neuren Sprachen und Literaturen*, 211 (1974) 31-44.

10 On the way the relationship of Angel Clare and Liza-Lu forms a kind of 'new marriage', see Jan B. Gordon, 'Origins, History, and the Reconstitution of Family: Tess's Journey', *Thomas Hardy*, ed. Harold Bloom (New York: Chelsea House Publishers, 1987), pp. 115-135.

11 See Alan Friedman, *The Turn of the Novel* (New York: Oxford University Press, 1966), pp. 71-74; Daniel R. Schwarz, 'Beginnings and Endings in Hardy's

Major Fiction' in *Critical Approaches to the Fiction of Thomas Hardy*, ed. by Dale Kramer (London: Macmillan, 1979), pp. 33-34; Peter Casagrande, *Unity in Hardy's Novels: 'Repetitive Symmetries'* (London: Macmillan, 1982), p. 203; and David Sonstroem, 'Order and Disorder in *Jude the Obscure*', *English Literature in Transition*, 24 (1981), p. 9.

12 All references to the text of *Jude the Obscure* are to the Wessex Edition (London: Macmillan, 1912) and are indicated parenthetically by part numbers in Roman numerals followed by chapter numbers in Arabic numerals.

13 Fernand Lagarde's 'A propos de la construction de *Jude the Obscure*', *Caliban*, 3 (January, 1966), 185-214, argues -- mistakenly, I think -- for a pattern of rising hopes in the first four parts of the novel and only then declining, rather than the pattern of persistent and inexorable decline I point to in my analysis.

14 See Alan Friedman, *The Turn of the Novel* (New York: Oxford University Press, 1966); Beverley Gross, 'Narrative Time and the Open-ended Novel', *Criticism*, 8 (1966), 362-76; Frank Kermode, *The Sense of an Ending* (New York: Oxford University Press, 1967); David H. Richter *Fables' End: Completeness and Closure in Rhetorical Fiction* (Chicago and London: University of Chicago Press, 1974); and Maria Torgovnick, *Closure in the Novel* (Princeton: Princeton University Press, 1981), pp. 202-204.

15 Torgovnick, p. 206; see also Richter, pp. 2-7.

16 See, for example, Anthony Newcomb's analysis in 'Schumann and Late Eighteenth-Century Narrative Strategies', *Nineteenth-Century Music*, 11 (Fall, 1987), 164-174.

17 John Warrack, *Tchaikovsky* (London: Hamish Hamilton, 1973), p. 266.

18 Michael Millgate, *Thomas Hardy: A Biography* (New York: Random House, 1982), p. 448.

19 See, for example, Donal Henahan, 'The Going-Nowhere Music -- And Where it Came From', *New York Times*, Section 2, Arts and Leisure, Sunday, December 6, 1981, pp. 1, 25.

20 Thomas Hardy, *The Life and Work of Thomas Hardy*, ed. by Michael Millgate (London: Macmillan, 1984), p. 183, 192, 239.

21 August Strindberg, *To Damascus I, in Eight Expressionist Plays by August Strindberg*, translated by Arvid Paulson (New York: New York University Press, 1972) pp. 140-141.

22 The confusing use of the term *impressionism* in early twentieth-century painting is partly sorted out in Victor H. Miesel's 'The Term Expressionism in

the Visual Arts (1911-1920)', ed. by Hayden V. White, *The Uses of History: Essays in Intellectual and Social History Presented to William J. Bossenbrook* (Detroit MI: Wayne State University Press, 1968), pp. 135-152.

23 Examples of the Munch works referred to are all in the Munch Museum, Oslo, and are reproduced in Arne Eggum's *Edvard Munch: Paintings, Sketches, and Studies*, trans. by Ragnar Christophersen (New York: Clarckson N. Potter, Inc., 1984), illus. nos. 7, 12, and 238.

24 Reinhold Heller, *Edvard Munch: The Scream* (New York: Vicking Press, 1973), p. 23.

25 Edward Lockspeiser, *Music and Painting: A Study in Comparative Ideas from Turner to Schoenberg* (New York: Harper and Row, 1973), p. 133.

26 Quoted in R.S. Furness, *Expressionism* (London: Methuen and Co., 1973), p. 4.

27 Michael Millgate, *Thomas Hardy: His Career as a Novelist* (New York: Random House, 1971), p. 323.

28 For a differing view, particularly with respect to the realism of Hardy's treatment of Sue Bridehead, see Phillip Mallett, 'Sexual Ideology and Narrative Form in *Jude the Obscure*', *English*, 38 (Autumn, 1989) 211-224.

29 Hardy to Edmund Gosse, November 20, 1895, in Richard Little Purdy and Michael Millgate, eds., *The Collected Letters of Thomas Hardy: Volume II 1893-1901* (Oxford: Clarendon Press, 1980), p. 99.

30 See, for example, the review by Jeannette L. Gilder titled 'Hardy the Degenerate', *World*, 13 (November, 1895), 15 and, also, the comments by Edmund Gosse and R.Y. Tyrrell recorded in R. G. Cox's *Thomas Hardy: The Critical Heritage* (London: Routledge, 1970) pp. 266 and 293.

31 Hardy recorded passages from English translations of Zola's *Abbé Mouret's Transgressions* and from *Germinal* in his '1876' notebook; see *The Literary Notes of Thomas Hardy* ed. by Lennart Björk (Goteborg: Acta Universitatis Gothoburgensis, 1974), I, 403-405 and II, 189-191.

32 Emile Zola, *Correspondence* (Paris: F. Bernouard, 1928-29), letter of the lst of June, 1887, p. 679. On the way *En Rade* represents a movement from naturalism to a more 'expressionist' kind of art, see Ruth B. Antosh, 'J.-K. Huysmans' *En Rade*: L'Enigme Resolue', *Bulletin de la Société J.-K. Huysmans*, 23 (1987), 33-43.

33 Hardy, *The Life and Work of Thomas Hardy*, p. 272.

34 Henrik Ibsen, *The Oxford Ibsen*, Vol. VII, ed. James Walter McFarlane, with translations by Jens Arp and James Walter MacFarlane (London: Oxford University Press, 1966), p. 432.

35 Charles Ives, *Variations on 'America' (1891) for Organ/'Adeste Fidelis' in an Organ Prelude (1897)* (New York: Music Press, 1949); this very early use of bi-tonality is notable particularly in the 'interlude' of measures 75-90. However, on p. [ii] an unsigned 'Note' to this edition suggests that the 'interlude' was not composed by 1891 but added some years later, and the subsequent questions raised by Maynard Solomon in 'Charles Ives: Some Questions of Veracity', *Journal of the American Musicological Society*, 40 (Fall, 1987), 443-470, do not increase confidence in the earlier date.

36 See, for example, J. Deroux, 'La Musique polytonale', *La Revue musicale*, 1921 (no. 11) and 1923 (no. 4), and A. Machabey, 'Disonance, polytonalité, and atonalite', *La Revue musicale*, 1931 (no. 116).

37 Joan Grundy, *Hardy and the Sister Arts* (London: The Macmillan Press, 1979), p. 66.

John Robert Cozens in Italy

'Cousins was all poetry' -- John Constable

Those ink and wash and watercolour views
Of palace, church or Claude-glass distant vale
Might seem, at first, stiff Models of Good Taste;
But 'Cousins was all poetry' as well.

For all their calm, their tact of tint and tone,
With nascent feelings, look, his landscapes stir;
The sun which breaks through clouds on *Naples Bay*,
Or *Villa d'Este* or *Arricia*.

So academic set-piece harmonies
Of Empire, Golden Age and Pastoral
Come charged through his imagining and touch
With first light glows of mood you could call Soul:

Restrained but luminous, his works surprise,
A Newfoundland of sense, new earth, new skies.

John Sell Cotman at Rokeby

If faith can move mountains, so then can art --
As in Cotman's two *Views* of Greta Bridge:
The first features sky where the second, instead,
Shows a rugged blue-shadowed fellside ridge.

All art is selection, as Cotman knew well,
At work on each similar, different scene,
With bogus blue hills for harmony's sake
Or counterfeit sky where hills should have been.

Almighty cheek or rank inconsistency
Or just artist's licence? The verdict depends
On *mimesis*, of course; how far can you go
Shunting landscape round as a means to your ends?

What magical weeks, though; Cotman at Rokeby;
What freshness and rightness of touch and of eye;
When 'ficle Dame Nature' was changed and improved
(Her sky turned to fellside, fellside to sky),

Was it faith of a sort, since a spirit had moved?

Colleague

Our colleague, Ernest Young, expounds
  To first year 'kids' upon
Metadiegetic discourse
  In Dickens and in Donne.

He thinks he'll make a chair before
  He's thirty-eight or so;
His latest work is due out soon
  On Methuen Video.

Archaic bourgeois structures must
  Dictate a bourgeois text:
That methodology once grasped,
  It's hermeneutics next.

He's a brand-new desk computer
  For poems he takes to bits.
'The author's dead', you understand;
  In his place our Ernest sits.

Evergreen

It's strange when you think of it, just how few
Poems in journal, quarterly or review
Draw on the Bible or *Book of Common Prayer*.
I mean, you'd imagine poets might still care
To conserve those wellsprings, not let them go dry,
And respect all that those old resonances signify.
But the everlasting waters have ebbed to what seems drought,
And the Tree of Knowledge looks to be grubbed out --
To adapt the new language of ecology
To that shared Christian legacy.
Why, in the stained glass of Chartres Cathedral, the rood
Is green-coloured always, for Grace and life renewed.

SIMON CURTIS

65

'The adventure to the unknown': Hardy, Lawrence and developments in the Novel

Rosemary Sumner

'Human character changed in 1910', said Virginia Woolf. [1] The precision of her dating was jokey and provocative but it was prompted by the first Post-Impressionist Exhibition in London, which took place that year and which showed, she felt, that ways of perceiving had irrevocably changed. Of course, she knew perfectly well that it wasn't as abrupt as this, and indeed, one may hesitate to describe a change in perception as a change in character. But changes certainly were going on. As early as 1887 Hardy's comments on the 'mad, late-Turner rendering' suggested different ways of looking: 'I want to see the deeper reality underlying the scenic, the expression of what are sometimes called abstract imaginings'. [2] Lawrence, too, thought artists were introducing innovative ways of seeing; on Cézanne he wrote: 'the eye sees only fronts, and the mind, on the whole, is satisfied with fronts. But intuition needs all-around-ness and instinct needs insideness. The true imagination is for ever curving round to the other side, to the back of the presented appearance.'[3]

I think one could trace the beginnings of the change, as it affected the novel, some forty years earlier than Woolf's proposed date, in Hardy's quite early novels. This essay will explore how these tendencies developed in Hardy's work and -- one might say -- exploded in Lawrence's central novels, *The Rainbow* and *Women in Love*. I'm going to focus on the fiction of both writers. Lawrence's 'Study of Thomas Hardy' is obviously central to the relationship between them and it will be implicit in what I say, but I am not planning to approach it directly, partly because it has already been discussed by a number of critics, and partly because I am more concerned with discerning a tendency than showing an influence. I see this tendency developing in Hardy and leading to the kind of modern novel Lawrence wrote (in contrast to the Joycean kind of modernism) and continuing in the works of Woolf and Beckett.

Fundamental to the change in modes of perceiving was the recognition of, or even confrontation with the unknown and unknowable. After the mid-nineteenth century scientific discoveries which enlarged conceptions of time and space almost beyond comprehension, 'the relationship between man and his circumambient universe' necessarily becomes a focus of attention in literature and art: Lawrence said it was 'the business of art'. [4] Of course, from the days of myth literature has been concerned with humanity's place in the cosmos, but the novel in its eighteenth- and nineteenth-century form had been primarily concerned with personal and social relationships, rather than with cosmic ones. When the boundaries of the universe recede into the unknown, the artist's subjects and forms must become more indeterminate. Hardy said, 'I am utterly bewildered to understand how the doctrine that beyond the knowable, there must always be an unknown, can be displaced'. [5]

Both novelists are making 'the adventure into the unknown'. This takes several forms. First there is their exploration of the characters' place in the expanding universe; then there is the world within, also expanding as awareness of subconscious and unconscious areas increases. As a result of this, novelists begin to create characters which cannot be wholly understood, even by their author and, of course, each character becomes an 'unknown mode of being' to the other characters. All this entails a feeling of uncertainty and danger which is heightened as late nineteenth- and early twentieth-century writing inevitably veers towards the taboo areas of the instincts, of sexuality, of the relationship between mind and body. Clearly, new forms, new ways of using language were needed if the novel were, even tentatively, to explore these aspects of life. And this is what Hardy did, tentatively feeling his way towards writing about the instincts and the unconscious, challenging the taboos, seeking a form which was indeterminate, inconclusive, preparing a way for Lawrence's reckless leap into the unknown. As a result, *Jude* was in danger of being banned, and of course *The Rainbow* was banned.

It is illuminating to take a detailed look at two opening chapters, of *The Return of the Native* (1878) and of *The Rainbow* (1915). There are no characters in the ordinary sense in either chapter. In *The Return of the Native* there is a hypothetical furzecutter who is aware of the light in the sky and the darkness of the heath and there is a 'mind' 'harassed by the irrepressible New' to which the heath is said to 'give ballast'. The first chapter of *The Rainbow* is similarly abstract, though more thickly populated with unnamed generations of Brangwens, stretching back into the past -- the ancestors of the characters of the novel. Hardy's timespan is longer than Lawrence's, for he goes back before humanity to 'the finger touches of the last geological change'. Yet, as with this image of 'finger touches' (instead of just saying 'marks'), he continually aligns this ancient, mysterious region (the word 'obscure' echoes through the chapter) with humanity. The heath is 'like man, colossal and enduring'. Most significantly, it connects with our unconscious: 'it was found to be the hitherto unrecognised original of those wild regions of obscurity which are vaguely felt to be compassing us about in midnight dreams of flight and disaster, and are never thought of after the dream till revived by scenes like this.' The stress is on the heath's correspondence to the most obscure and frightening levels of the unconscious, yet, paradoxically, it 'gives ballast' to the conscious mind. This recognition that when the conscious mind is in touch with unconscious impulses there is a stabilising effect is a mark of Hardy's psychological insight. As the novel develops he shows the dislocation caused by Eustacia's conscious hatred of the heath and her unconscious affinity with it. Yet, eventually, on her way to her death, she achieves an ironic kind of balance: 'Never was harmony more perfect than that between the chaos of her mind and the chaos of the world without.'

Lawrence, too, is concerned with how consciousness and the unconscious relate to the cosmos and to time. The long generations of Brangwens look 'as if they were expecting something unknown'. Though they participate in the cycle of the seasons ('They felt the rush of sap in spring, they knew the wave that cannot halt, but every year throws forward the seed to begetting'), and they know the closeness of their relationship to the earth ('they felt the pulse and body of the soil'), Lawrence also says that they are 'staring into the sun'. Attention is usually drawn to the men turned towards the earth and the women looking to the horizon -- a limited, social horizon. But it is important that the Marsh folk combine their earth-bound vision with a cosmic one, in this way indicating the potential for development in *The Rainbow* and *Women in Love*. Their position in relation to the universe is similar to that of Hardy's hypothetical observer on the heath. Both are attuned to the continuing cycle of nature and open to the shock of the unknown beyond the earth or in the psyche.

Hardy described the setting of his novels as 'partly real, partly dream-country'. Egdon Heath is 'real' in the sense that it is 'made vividly visible'; it is 'dream-country' in that it represents the movements of the mind, both of the conscious mind and of the obscure and inapprehensible unconscious. Lawrence, in *The Rainbow*, simultaneously gives a swift and vivid impression of the year's work on the farm and conveys the inner life of the men who 'lived full and surcharged, their sense full-fed....impregnated with the day, cattle and earth and vegetation and the sky'. In these two chapters we see the move away from the novel's traditional sphere of human relationships to a new direction evoked by Virginia Woolf in her essay 'The Narrow Bridge of Art'; she says the new novel 'will give the relation of the mind to general ideas and its soliloquy in solitude...for an important part of life consists in our emotions towards such things as roses and nightingales, the dawn, the sunset, life, death and fate.' [6]

She felt that this new thing probably could not be called a novel. She need not have been so tentative. Hardy and Lawrence had got there before her and she admitted that the novel can 'take in contrasting and incongruous things'. Her 'new novel' would resemble poetry, she said. Thirty years earlier, in 1897, Hardy said he had aimed at keeping his narratives 'as near to poetry in their subject as the conditions would allow'. [7] These opening chapters of *The Return* and *The Rainbow* are written in markedly rhythmic prose. Both novelists are moving away from the tradition of realism in nineteenth-century fiction, with 'its marvellous fact-recording power' (Woolf again) towards a mode which does indeed resemble poetry: 'the sea changed, the fields changed, the rivers, the villages and the people changed, yet Egdon remained.' The suggestion of incantation is even more marked in *The Rainbow*: 'They took the udders of the cows, the cows yielded milk and pulse against the hands of the men, the pulse of the blood of the teats of the cows beat into the pulse of the hands of the men.' This emphatically onomatopoeic rhythm, which would be conventional in a poem, illustrates Woolf's point that there need be no clear-cut distinction between fiction and poetry.

But neither of them is writing quite the kind of novel Woolf envisaged. The second chapter of both novels makes an abrupt switch to traditional modes of story-telling. Hardy's Chapter Two starts: 'Along the road walked an old man'; Lawrence's Chapter Two: 'About 1840 a canal was constructed across the meadows'. The precision and limitation of place and time indicate that (for the moment at least) we have moved to a more manageable, more easily apprehensible world.

These transitions from one mode of perceiving and writing to another are characteristic of both of them. In the Preface to *Two on a Tower*, Hardy writes of setting 'the emotional history of two infinitesimal lives against the stupendous background of the stellar universe' and he suggests that to readers 'the smaller might be the greater to them as men'. Lawrence said the opposite; he found in Hardy, 'a great background, vital and vivid, which matters more than the people who move upon it.' However, trusting the tale rather than the teller (or the critic) I would say that the interest lies in the way the background and the human lives are related. In *Two on a Tower* the characters find themselves 'plunging' among the stars by means of Swithin's telescope, the 'mind feeling its way through a heaven of total darkness, occasionally striking against the black invisible cinders of stars'; they are 'aware of a vastness they could not cope with, even as an idea'. By juxtaposing these terrifying experiences of infinite space to the tender emotions of the lovers, Hardy heightens both our sense of human littleness and vulnerability and our fear of contemplating an endless void. Yet this sense of the precariousness of life makes it all the more powerful and precious in the face of annihilation.

In *Tess*, Hardy briefly makes a similar juxtapositon when he brings into the field at Flintcomb-Ash the 'strange birds from behind the North Pole' which have 'witnessed scenes of cataclysmal horror in inaccessible polar regions of a magnitude such as no human being had ever conceived, in curdling temperatures no man could endure.'[9] As in *Two on a Tower*, he exposes the reader to a place beyond human conception. Using appropriately polysyllabic language to suggest an overwhelming vastness, he sets this against the 'homely upland', the girls hacking swedes and the birds which are now merely looking for food. A sense of the inapprehensible is brought sharply into the context of the everyday life of farmworkers. The reader's response to both the inconceivable and the ordinary is vivified by the juxtaposition.

Lawrence often works in the same way. In *Sons and Lovers* he jumps from a quarrel (an everyday event in the Morel family) to the strangeness of the night-time garden as Mrs. Morel, locked out, becomes aware first of the 'glistening great rhubarb leaves' (weird, almost menacing in the darkness), then of 'the immense gulf of white light' and 'the tall white lilies reeling in the moonlight'. When Walter at last unlocks the door, 'there stood the silver-grey night, fearful to him' but Mrs. Morel is back at once into daily routine, putting his pit clothes ready and so on. [9] These non-human modes of being are all the more powerful because they co-exist with the realistically portrayed everyday life of the Morels. Both writers make us stare into space, contemplate nothingness and meaninglessness. Hardy said, 'Courage has been idealised; why not Fear? -- which is a higher consciousness, and based on a deeper insight.' [10]

This 'higher consciousness' and 'deeper insight' is evident in the way they both confront death. In *The Woodlanders* Giles is dying, delirious, alone in the wood. Grace, in the hut, hears something she thinks might be a squirrel or a bird; then it becomes 'an endless monologue, like that we sometimes hear from inanimate nature in deep secret places where water flows or where ivy flaps against stones'. [11] So, in his process towards death, Giles becomes first part of the animal world, then of the inanimate world of water, wind and stone. Personality has gone now. 'Autumn's very brother' who was both an abstraction and a warm, living human being, has become simply an element in a lonely elemental place. But the process of dying is not completed. Hardy goes further into non-human, unknown regions. The delirious murmur becomes 'like a comet, erratic, inapprehensible, untraceable'. It is strange to see a man as a comet, and the adjectives -- erratic (and so unpredictable), inapprehensible, untraceable -- are negative and abstract. With this imaginative leap into outer space, with these negatives and abstractions, Giles leaves this world and makes his transition to what Lawrence called 'the pure inhuman otherness of death'. But, oddly, Giles is not yet dead. Hardy does a strange thing here. After this flight into death, he gives another 'realistic', traditional death scene in the hut, registered in terms of the consciousness of Grace and Fitzpiers (whereas the 'comet' episode, ostensibly emanating from Grace's consciousness, seems to move away from her and become impersonal). This traditional treatment of death is quiet and not very disturbing. Fitzpiers says Giles's extremities are already dead and that his previous illness was likely to be followed by a relapse anyway, thus making the death seem normal and expected and therefore less disquieting. The 'comet' image gives an utterly different view of death. These two scenes illustrate Hardy's capacity to be a nineteenth- and a twentieth-century writer simultaneously. The gap between the two modes of perceiving is enormous. In these gaps the imagination is suddenly thrust out of its normal tracks to contemplate non-human modes of being; here we encounter 'the intenser stare of the mind'. [12]

There are similar shifts in Lawrence. In *Sons and Lovers*, Mrs. Morel's death is presented first in precise, exact and agonising detail as Paul experiences its slow advance. Apart from the horror of the clinical detail, it is in the tradition of nineteenth-century deathbeds. At the end of the novel, Paul experiences it again. This time it is not the process, but the fact of death. He faces 'everywhere the vastness and terror of the night...There was no Time, only Space...the immense dark silence seemed pressing him into extinction...she was gone, intermingled herself.' [13] As in Hardy, the domestic, factual, traditional scene is contrasted with vastness and space and extinction. But, here, the reader is aware all the time of observing Paul's consciousness -- this is the centre of interest. In *The Woodlanders*, when Giles becomes 'inapprehensible, untraceable', Grace's consciousness is no longer our concern -- the focus is on the voyage into space. In both novels the 'abstract imaginings' occur in contexts which are mainly traditional and realistic. Thus, at the end of *The Woodlanders*, when she is mourning over Giles's grave, Hardy attributes to Marty the 'quality of abstract humanism'. Yet that final elegy, celebrating Giles's life, also outlines Marty's future: 'Whenever I plant the young larches, I'll think that none can plant as you planted...' [14] In Marty's dirge the abstraction of universal mourning co-exists with a move back from outer space and the unknown to the everyday and the known. Lawrence makes a similar movement as Paul rejects 'the drift towards death': 'But no, he would not give in...he walked towards the faintly humming, glowing town, quickly.' [15]

These tentative moves back from the unknown to somewhat more manageable and reassuring aspects of existence are rejected in the later books of both authors. Round Jude's death Hardy creates a gap, a silence juxtaposed to explosions of colour and noise. Jude seems to efface himself, to create a state of not being. His own last words are, 'And I here. And Sue defiled.' The elliptical 'And I here', the absence of any verb 'to be' preempts the actual moment of death. Like Tess, he'd 'have his life unbe'. This is followed by the murmured quotations from *Job* in which Jude's own first person 'I' is subsumed under that of Job. The yells from the races cut across the Biblical words. These abrupt interruptions from 'the many and strong' are reinforced by the bigger narrative gap as Hardy switches with equal abruptness to Arabella looking for amusement in town. The jerky cross-cutting from death to a particularly brash and callous form of life continues. The moment of death is left as a gap -- unstated. Arabella returns to find Jude's body still warm: 'She listened at his chest. All was still within. The bumping of near thirty years had ceased.' Immediately there's the sound of a brass band and Arabella's exclamations of annoyance at this interruption to her day's pleasure. Hardy's language creates an explosion of noise and colour: 'The gay barges burst on the view, the oars smacking with a loud kiss on the face of the stream' -- even the oars join in the rowdiness with their vulgar, loud-mouthed, 'smacking kiss'. There are 'gorgeous nosegays of feminine beauty in green, pink, blue and white' and a loud, red-uniformed brass band. Later, as Jude lies in his coffin, there are cheers from the degree ceremony and bells 'struck out joyously and travelled round the bedroom'. [16] In this cutting from the noise of life to the silence of death, Hardy is creating, in a way quite different from that of *The Woodlanders*, a sense of 'the pure inhuman otherness of death'.

The resemblances to 'In Tenebris II' (written the year after *Jude*) show again the movement of the novel towards poetry. The 'stout upstanders' like Arabella will carry on, while Jude is 'one born out of due time, who has no calling here'. [17] *Jude the Obscure*, like Lawrence's poetry, is 'inconclusive'. The unstated death, the indefinite future for Sue prevent a positive conclusion. Even Arabella's apparently confident comment on Sue is oddly circumlocutory, looking into the future and then turning back on itself, 'till she's as he is now'.

Gerald's 'snow-abstract annihilation' at the end of *Women in Love* is a further exploration of the 'otherness' of death. The gleaming ice imagery which has been associated with Gerald all through the book reaches its culmination here; his estrangement from life is embodied in the landscape of white snow slopes and black rock, the immense height, remote from all living things, the sound-lessness. 'How frail a thread of his being was stretched' suggests a state similar to the elliptical 'And·I here' in *Jude*. And, as in *Jude*, the exact moment of death goes unstated: 'He slipped and fell down and as he fell, something broke in his soul and he immediately went to sleep.' [18] A few lines later, in the next chapter, on the next morning, Gudrun is told that he died 'hours ago'. His transition from being scarcely conscious to being 'so inert, so coldly dead, a carcass' happens in the space between chapters 30 and 31, just as Jude's death occurs between the last words quoted from *Job* and Arabella's return.

Gerald had willed the finality of death, he had 'wanted to go on, to the end. Never again to stay, till he came to the end', and the 'coldly dead' carcass seems utterly final. But Lawrence does not use this death to make a Victorian ending, rounding things off; he makes it indeterminate. Birkin, meditating on it, thinks of impermanence, of how humanity could die out and be replaced by 'a finer created being'. And even Gerald, now 'an inert mass', could have responded to Birkin's offered love; then he could have 'lived still in the beloved', an idea Birkin tentatively offers to Ursula as possible for the two of them. [19] The novel evades finality. It ends -- breaks off -- in the middle of a conversation. It is as inconclusive as a novel could be. As Lawrence said of his poetry, 'incon-clusiveness, immediacy, the quality of life itself, without denouement or close....none of that finality which we find so satisfying because we are so frightened'. [20] These two novelists confront this fear, refuse to contain it or to console.

Inconclusiveness, indeterminacy, the unknown, the abstract are features of twentieth century arts -- one thinks of the moves towards abstraction in painting or in electronic music, of Stockhausen, for instance, who said that when he was incorporating sounds from the air waves in his music, he felt as if he were in communication with the cosmos. Perhaps these qualities would not seem to fuse happily with the aspects of nineteenth-century realism which Hardy and Lawrence retained. Little Father Time is a challenging example. He has often been criticised as being overburdened with the symbolic weight put upon him. He is incongruous in a novel largely presented in terms of verisimili-tude. But Hardy was developing another kind of fiction, which, like Lawrence's, questioned conventional form. Little Father Time, appearing from nowhere, gazing with unearthly vision at the world around is similar to Golding's Matty in *Darkness Visible*, appearing out of the fire and carrying with him a strange burden of insight. Little Father Time views humanity with the remote compas-sion of the Spirit of the Pities in *The Dynasts*. He is not explained (apart from the doctor's portentous remark, which should, perhaps, be taken as Hardy's ironic comment on a scientific mind's 'irritable reaching after fact and reason'). Little Father Time is, like Sue, 'puzzling and unstateable'. Ian Gregor and Michael Irwin have written of 'the intensity of feeling behind his creation'. They say that *Jude* without Little Father Time would be a lesser novel, a tragedy not about the universe but about unfulfilled ambitions and domestic strife: 'Father Time marks the outermost reach of Hardy's art; the extravagance is too great, the stylisation fails; the formal and realistic modes collide...the very violence of that collision is a measure of [Hardy's] creative energy, of his undiminished eagerness to encompass something new.' [21]

I agree with almost all of this. But, having so movingly indicated the power of Little Father Time in the novel, having seen the 'creative energy' in the collision of modes, they draw back as if overwhelmed; the extravagance is 'too great', 'it fails'. Yet the whole point, as Gregor and Irwin show so vividly, is the violence of the incongruity. The juxtaposition of the symbolic with the realistic mode heightens the unease which the grotesque death scene arouses. It threatens to fragment the novel -- and this is the point. Hardy and Lawrence were exploring new perceptions; for their purpose a new kind of novel was necessary. Hardy created one in which it was possible for Little Father Time, with his 'impersonal quality, the movement of a wave or a breeze or a cloud', with his 'view over some great Atlantic of Time' and with his concern with 'the generals of life', [22] not the particulars, to have his place in a book partly dealing with topical issues such as the right to education and the iniquities of the marriage laws. But the strangeness of Little Father Time is only an extreme form of Hardy's sense of the inexplicable nature of human beings. As early as *Far from the Madding Crowd* he suggests the importance of unconscious drives in Boldwood's repression of earlier traumatic experiences, which, nonetheless, have left 'high water marks'. He calls Grace 'a conjectural creature'. And it is in *Jude the Obscure* that he confronts most explicitly the problem of conveying in words what is unknown to the conscious mind and therefore unarticulated. Sue has 'untranslatable eyes', [23] she is 'one lovely conundrum', [24] she is 'puzzling and unstateable'. [25] This word 'unstateable' is particularly significant. In the first edition it was 'unpredictable', which, while being accurate about Sue, did not touch on the problem facing the novelist. Hardy was well aware that the new novel required a new language. Language inevitably tends to run the risk of explaining the inexplicable, stating the unstateable. Hardy avoids this by creating a changing, inconsistent, contradictory, precariously balanced character, whom he then exposes to the traumatic experience of the deaths of the children. In her apparent *volte face* from sceptical rationalism to religious fanaticism Hardy is exploring further the areas of masochism and sexuality which he had indicated as problematic for her earlier in the novel. Lawrence (in his 'Study of Thomas Hardy') saw her as like Cassandra, asexual; he accepted Jude's momentary feeling that she was a specialised type and should not have been violated. The novel does not seem to me to endorse this; Hardy repeatedly seems to suggest that she has strong sexual feelings which she is afraid of and represses, perhaps just because they are so strong. Her use of imagery is suggestive; while arguing that Phillotson is her real husband, she says, 'I want to prick myself all over with pins to let out all the badness that is in me'. [26] These images of penetration, associated with pain and sin, may perhaps be seen as implying a masochistic sexuality. On Jude's last visit, she kisses him, saying, 'I give you back your kisses -- I do, I do -- and now I'll hate myself for ever for my sin'. [27] This certainly does not seem to suggest an absence of sexual feeling. Nor does her insistence on returning to Phillotson's bed with 'a look of aversion...but clenching her teeth she uttered no cry'; [28] rather it supports the idea of a terrifying sex-drive. Her relationships with men -- the undergraduate, Phillotson, Jude, Phillotson again -- parallel closely Arabella's sexual relationships -- with Jude, Mr. Cartlett, Jude again, Vilbert. The apparently sexless Sue is as good as sexy Arabella at getting herself into a position where a sexual relationship is at least possible. Hardy's tentative suggestions of these unconscious contradictions indicate that Jude the Obscure is taking fiction in new directions, into the uncertain, unknown world of the unconscious and the then taboo world of sexuality, while seeking a language and a form to express them.

The unconscious fear, even horror, of the self, which Hardy suggests in Sue, is something which Lawrence, too, explores, while going much further than Hardy in suggesting that violent and destructive impulses exist in all of us and don't need such traumatic experiences as the murder and suicide of children to account for them. Writing twenty years later than Hardy, Lawrence is able to recognise more fully the existence of the unconscious and to explore it more directly. Hardy uses dialogue, Sue's partially accurate self-analysis, Jude's bewilderment and incredulity to hint at what is going on beneath the surface. Even the narrator has no direct access to Sue's unconscious; her behaviour is described (her look of aversion and clenched teeth, for instance) and the reader draws conclusions from that. Hardy makes his point by leaving her as puzzling to readers as to herself and to the other characters.

Lawrence uses different methods for similar purposes. Like Hardy he is moving away from the notion that characters in novels should be fully known, fully explained. Even as late as 1927 in Aspects of the Novel Forster suggested that 'a character is real when the novelist knows everything about it...he may not choose to tell us all he knows...but he will give us the feeling that though the character has not been explained, it is explicable'. He even claimed that the virtue of novels is that 'they suggest a more comprehensible and manageable human race' and 'solace us' by giving us 'the illusion of perspicacity and power'. [29] (In justice to Forster, I must say in parenthesis that most of Aspects of the Novel and his fiction are far more complex than this.) Yet, that somebody of the stature and power of Forster as a novelist was able, so late in the day, to assume that it was the function of fiction to offer readers the explicable and illusions and solace serves to show how strongly Hardy and Lawrence had gone against the current of their time.

Hardy leaves the reader guessing about Sue. Lawrence in The Rainbow seems to do the opposite by giving the narrator direct access to the unconscious of the characters. But he always makes it clear that he is able to throw light on only a limited area for 'beyond the knowable there must always be an unknown'. A vivid and explicit example of Lawrence's methods is Ursula's terrifying experience during the dance by the stacks in The Rainbow. [30] He conveys the strangeness by starting with the universe: 'the great slow surging of the whole night...one great flood heaving slowly backwards to the verge of oblivion, slowly forward to the other verge'; then, with 'the heart sweeping along each time' the human element becomes part of the universal process. 'The whole night' and the heart become identified in their movement. This leads the way to Ursula's strange relationship with the moon: 'She was as bright as a piece of moonlight, bright as a steel blade, he seemed to be grasping a blade that hurt him.' The imagery becomes more and more surrealistic. Like Sue, Ursula 'was afraid of what she was'. After four pages of exploring her unconscious in strange imagery and hypnotic rhythms, Lawrence brings her back to what he calls 'daytime consciousness'. Like the reader, she is horrified. She is 'filled with overpowering fear of herself, overpowering desire that it should not be, that other burning, corrosive self...She denied it with all her might...She was good, she was loving..."Isn't it lovely?" she said softly, coaxingly, caressingly.' The shock of this transition heightens the disturbing strangeness of Lawrence's venture into the unconscious.

This contrasting of the unconscious with 'daytime consciousness' is an extreme form of the contrasts between the unknown and the known which I have been commenting on in the works of Hardy and Lawrence. After these strange and exciting experiments in *The Rainbow*, Lawrence developed further such contrasting methods in *Women in Love*. 'A truly perfect relationship is one in which each party leaves great tracts unknown in the other party', he said in *Studies in Classic American Literature*. Birkin tells Ursula, 'We are two stark unknown beings,' and she sees 'the dark subtle reality of him, never to be translated'. When they make love in Sherwood Forest, Lawrence wants to convey 'the sensual reality of that which can never be transmuted into mind content'. H. M. Daleski objects to this on the grounds that if the experience were 'untranslatable', then 'the attempt to render it in words was probably misguided anyway'. [34] I profoundly disagree with this, and so would have Hardy and Lawrence. Hardy said, 'when a man not contented with the grounds of his success goes on and on, and tries to achieve the impossible, then he gets profoundly interesting to me.' [35] Lawrence wrote, in the Foreword to *Women in Love*, 'Any man of real individuality tries to know and understand what is happening, even in himself, as he goes along. This struggle for verbal consciousness should not be left out in art. It is a very great part of life.' [36] The struggle is very evident in *Women in Love* with its frequent discussions about the difficulty and inadequacy of words to convey profound emotional experiences. Lawrence and Hardy were grappling with the same problem of articulating what is not experienced at a cognitive level. The repeated 'never to be translated' in *Women in Love* links it directly to *Jude the Obscure*, with Sue's 'untranslatable eyes' and 'unstateable' nature. Sue struggles to analyse herself, just as the characters in *Women in Love* seek for words to convey their inner experiences. The 'struggle for verbal consciousness' is central to both novels, while at the same time both novelists insist that there will always remain 'the unknowable beyond the known'. *Women in Love* is full of unanswered questions, abstractions, negatives. While there may, perhaps, be some slight justification for saying (as one critic has) that the 'procedures of *The Rainbow* don't offer enough for the cognitive imagination', [37] it is certainly not applicable to

Women in Love, which combines the compelling emotional power of *The Rainbow* with this appeal to the 'cognitive imagination'.

This combination connects with Lawrence's view that 'life is only bearable when the mind and the body are in harmony...and each has a natural respect for the other'. [38] Hardy thought so too, but, being a Victorian novelist, he was unable to express it so unequivocally. In *Tess* and *Jude* mind and body are split between two characters, Angel and Sue representing mind, Alec and Arabella representing body. Modern Hardy says of Angel: 'with more animalism he would have been a nobler man.' 'We do not say it', [39] Victorian Hardy hastily adds. Similarly, if Sue's intellect could have been combined with Arabella's sexuality in one person, then a happy relationship with Jude would have been possible, but to this kind of thing 'English society opposes a well-nigh insuperable bar', Hardy said in 'Candour in English Fiction'. [40] Though Tess and possibly Jude may have mind and body in harmony, they cannot be allowed a partner who is similarly balanced. Sexual happiness can only be momentary and doomed, as in the brief honeymoon in the house in the woods before Tess's capture at Stonehenge. Writing twenty years later, Lawrence can show Ursula progressing towards a state where mind and body are in harmony and she and Birkin can achieve, at least intermittently, a fulfilling relationship.

If character was indeed changing during the writing lives of Hardy and Lawrence (and certainly, if nothing else, attitudes to sex were changing), then their own writing made some contribution to that change and, of course, to the consequent changes in the novel form. In 1886, Hardy wrote, 'novel-writing as an art cannot go backward. Having reached the analytic stage it must transcend it by going further in the same direction. Why not by rendering as visible essences...the abstract thoughts of the analytic school?' [41] This move towards abstraction is a high risk strategy; like abstract art and experimental electronic music it may at first seem incomprehensible or pretentious. But Hardy and Lawrence refused to be confined by convention. Lawrence said, 'As a novelist, I feel it is the change inside the individual which is my concern...My field is to know the feelings inside a man and to make new feelings conscious.' [42] By their continual adventuring into the unknown, Hardy and Lawrence opened up new possibilities both for the novel and for human experience.

NOTES

1   Virginia Woolf, 'Mr. Bennett and Mrs. Brown', *Collected Essays*, 4 vols (London, 1966-67), I, 320.

2   *The Life and Work of Thomas Hardy*, ed. Michael Millgate (London, 1984), p. 192.

3 D.H. Lawrence, 'Introduction to these Paintings', in *Phoenix*, ed. E. McDonald (London, 1936), p. 579.

4 D.H. Lawrence, 'Morality and the Novel', in *Phoenix*, p. 579.

5 *The Life and Work of Thomas Hardy*, p. 400.

6 Virginia Woolf, 'The Narrow Bridge of Art', *Collected Essays*, II, 225.

7 *The Life and Work of Thomas Hardy*, p. 309.

8 *Tess of the d'Urbervilles*, chapter 43.

9 *Sons and Lovers*, chapter 1.

10 *The Life and Work of Thomas Hardy*, p. 269.

11 *The Woodlanders*, chapter 42.

12 'In Front of the Landscape', in *The Complete Poems of Thomas Hardy*, ed. James Gibson (London, 1976), pp. 303-5.

13 *Sons and Lovers*, chapter 15.

14 *The Woodlanders*, chapter 48.

15 *Sons and Lovers*, chapter 15.

16 *Jude the Obscure*, Part Sixth, XI.

17 *The Complete Poems of Thomas Hardy*, p. 168.

18 *Women in Love*, chapter 30.

19 *Women in Love*, chapter 31.

20 'Poetry of the Present', in *The Complete Poems of D.H. Lawrence*, ed. V. de S. Pinto and W. Roberts, 2 vols, 2nd ed. (London, 1967) I, 183-4.

21 'Either Side of Wessex', in Lance St. John Butler (ed.), *Thomas Hardy after Fifty Years* (London, 1977), p. 115.

22 *Jude the Obscure*, Part Fifth, III.

23 *Jude*, Part Second, II.

24 *Jude*, Part Third, I.

25 *Jude*, Part Fourth, III.

26 *Jude*, Part Sixth, III.

27 *Jude*, Part Sixth, VIII.

28 *Jude*, Part Sixth, IX.

29 E. M. Forster, *Aspects of the Novel* (London, 1927), chapter 3.

30 *The Rainbow*, chapter 11.

31 *Studies in Classic American Literature*, chapter 10.

32 *Women in Love*, chapter 13.

33 *Women in Love*, chapter 23.

34 Peter Preston and Peter Hoare (eds), *D.H. Lawrence in the Modern World*, (Basingstoke, 1988), p. 94.

35 *The Life and Work of Thomas Hardy*, p. 354.

36 D.H. Lawrence, in *Phoenix II*, ed. W. Roberts and Harry T. Moore (London, 1968), p. 276.

37 See Jacques Berthoud, 'The Rainbow as an Experimental Novel', in A.H. Gomme (ed), *D.H. Lawrence: a critical study* (Brighton, 1978), pp. 53-69.

38 *A Propos of 'Lady Chatterley's Lover'*, 1929 (Harmondsworth, 1961), p. 92.

39 *Tess of the d'Urbervilles*, chapter 36.

40 *Thomas Hardy's Personal Writings*, ed. H. Orel (Lawrence, Kansas, 1966), p. 128.

41 *The Life and Work of Thomas Hardy*, p. 183.

42 *Phoenix II*, p. 567.

Hardy's *The Well-Beloved,* Sex, and Theories of Germ Plasm

J. B. Bullen

The Well-Beloved resembles *The Tempest*. Like Shakespeare's play, it is set mainly on an island which is palpable and physical, yet at the same time exists in the realm of the imagination. Like Prospero, Hardy's hero, Jocelyn Pierston, has a life which is divided between a public career on a distant mainland and a fantastic, insular world of the mind. Young women of the island dominate both men's lives: in Prospero's case it is his daughter Miranda, in Pierston's it is the three Avice Caro girls, and both stories are concerned with the role of nature and nurture in human behaviour. The correspondences do not end there, extending even to the relationship between author and text. Prospero is an artist in magic, Pierston an artist in stone, and their renunciation of their two arts corresponds to their creators' farewells to their respective métiers. Prospero buries his staff three fathoms deep, and Shakespeare writes no more. Pierston 'sees no more to move him' [1] in the National Gallery, and with the 'extinction of the Well-Beloved' closes 'the natural fountains' (205) on his mental island. And 'so ended,' wrote Hardy, his own 'prose contributions to literature.'[2]

Hardy said that he gave up novel writing as the result of adverse, even abusive criticism, and he affected amazement at the accusation of 'sex mania' levelled at him on the appearance of *The Well-Beloved* first in serial form in 1892, then in 1897. [3] The story of a man who pursues a woman, then her daughter, and at the age of sixty-one is making up to her nineteen-year-old granddaughter may not be politically correct, but hardly merits 'two years hard' at Her Majesty's pleasure, as one of Hardy's critics recommended. [4] Though Hardy put his subject more delicately -- he called it 'a subjective theory of love' [5] -- 'sex mania' is in fact a more accurate term because this story is about sex before it is about love. But it is about sex in the deepest sense. It is about sex as one of life's ruling passions; sex as the spring of thought and action, sex as the force which drives creativity and which defies the dictates of reason, and sex as the fertile breeding ground for the more delicate and acceptable flowers of love.

In spite, however, of the stress on the embodiment of sexual desire, and in spite of what appears to be the persistent womanizing of the hero: in spite, too, of the obsession of the sculptor with the female body and his susceptibility to appearances, this is not a sensual book. The various Avices have nothing of the coquetry of Fancy Day, the torrid heat of Eustacia Vye, the languorous voluptuousness of Tess, or the earthiness of Arabella Donn. Pierston is no Don Juan and, scarcely aware of their own desirability, the island girls are not *femmes fatales*. In the earlier novels, Hardy had explored many of the behavioural mechanisms of sexuality, together with its physical and psychological manifestations; but in this story, he explores sexuality at another level and in doing so moves towards the very bedrock of the processes of human reproduction. This might seem a bold claim had Hardy not given us a clue to the true nature of his subject when he directed our attention to a riddling poem entitled 'Heredity'. [6] It runs:

I am the family face;
Flesh perishes, I live on,
Projecting trait and trace
Through time to times anon,
And leaping from place to place
Over oblivion.

The years-heired feature that can
In curve and voice and eye
Despise the human span
Of durance -- that is I;
The eternal thing in man,
That heeds no call to die. [7]

The answer to the riddle is what Hardy's contemporaries called 'gemmules' or 'germ plasm' [8] and which we now know as the genetically regulative mechanisms in the cell structure. The sentiments of the poem derive from Hardy's reading in hereditary theory, and particularly a remark by Johannes Müller who said: 'Organic bodies are perishable; while life maintains the appearance of immortality in the constant succession of similar individuals, the individuals themselves pass away.' [9] In *The Well-Beloved*, the bodies of two of the Avice's 'pass away', while their sexual characteristics are passed on by heredity from mother to daughter to granddaughter. Indeed, the special characteristics of the inhabitants of the 'Isle of Slingers' -- their voices, their gestures and movements, and above all their physical appearances -- derive from what Hardy calls 'some mysterious ingredient sucked from the isle' (89) living on 'through time to times anon'. 'Johannes Müller is right,' said August Weismann, one of the specialist writers whom Hardy was reading in 1890, 'when he speaks of an appearance of immortality which passes from each individual into that which succeeds it'; [10] the 'undying part of the organism' he added, 'is the germ-plasm'. Pierston, too, is bound into this hereditary pattern since he shares the biological inheritance of the island inhabitants, 'a descendant of wreckers and smugglers.' (118)

But this is only half the story, because 'The eternal thing in man', That heeds no call to die' cannot exist in isolation and is intimately dependent for its perpetuation upon sexual selection and sexual desire. Hardy knew as well as we do that the gene is selfish. As humans we may have romanticized that selfishness, and in such figures as Romeo and Juliet, Tristan and Isolde, and Antony and Cleopatra have humanized and individualized it. But as Darwin and others in the nineteenth century pointed out, the gene is concerned for the future of the race or the species, not the well-being or fulfillment of the individual. So in *The Well-Beloved*, Pierston, no heartless philanderer, is driven on genetically to find an appropriate mate, admitting that his Beloved 'has had many incarnations -- too many to describe in detail,' and where 'Each shape, or embodiment, has been a temporary residence only...' (54) Consequently, as he discusses his laundry with the second Avice, he 'was thinking of the girl, or as the scientific might say, Nature was working her plans for the next generation under the cloak of a dialogue on linen.' (102) Pierston's is indeed a kind of 'sex mania'; it is a 'doom' or 'curse' (154), and Hardy knew as well as Freud how it dominated human behaviour in such a way that even at the age of sixty-one Pierston is 'urged on and on like the Jew Ahasuerus -- or, in the phrase of the islanders themselves, like a blind ram.' (154)

Hardy lends the genetic impulse greater intensity by his choice of location within an endogamous island community. The term 'endogamous' was first suggested by J. F. McLennan in his book *Primitive Marriage* (1865), where it describes tribes in which all the members are 'of the same blood, or feigning themselves to be so'; where there is 'Connubium between members of the tribe' and where 'marriage without the tribe is forbidden or punished.' [11] It is an updated version of this system which prevails on the Isle of Slingers. John Brand in his *Observations on Popular Antiquities* points out that such conditions still prevailed on nineteenth-century Portland. He is discussing 'Handefasting' -- the tradition of sexual intercourse and pregnancy before marriage which Hardy describes as 'the formal ratification of a betrothal, according to the precedent of their sires and grandsires' (37) -- and quotes from a document of 1543 which says that 'two handfested personnes [are] brought and layed together, yea certain wekes afore they go to the Chyrch.' [12] 'I was assured,' Brand continues, 'by credible authority on Portland Island that something very like it is still practised there very generally, where the inhabitants seldom or never intermarry with any one on the mainland and where young women, selecting lovers of the same place, account it no disgrace to allow them every favour, too, from the fullest confidence of being made wives the moment such consequences of their stolen embraces become too visible for further concealment.' [13] So, when the second Avice tells Pierston about her name -- 'my second name is [Avice] And my surname is [Caro]. Poor mother married her cousin' -- Pierston promptly replies: 'As everybody does here.' (95) For this reason Pierston, 'for ... lack of this groundwork of character', is unable to love 'a woman other than of the island race', there being, according to the author, 'a racial instinct necessary to the absolute unison of a pair.' (89) In this way Hardy strengthens the sense of anthropological determinism by suggesting that not merely custom, but genetic propensity is responsible for the endogamy of the small family groups in this community.

As both Hardy's poem and contemporary writing on genetics make clear, hereditary forces are not personal and individual, but lie outside and beyond the beings that are their vehicles. In *The Well-Beloved* the feeling of impersonality is enhanced through Hardy's extended use of the island setting and most particularly of the rock of which it is composed. The soaring 'infinitely stratified walls of oolite' (28) extend upwards from the non-human world into the habitations of man, which in turn, pile one upon the other: 'one man's doorstep rising behind his neighbour's chimney' (28). The rock is a record of the passing of time -- of geological time and then, when fashioned into building material, of historical time: 'Norman, Anglian, Roman, Balearic-British.' (89) In this way the antiquity of the rock provides an emblem for the immortal 'germ plasm' -- 'The eternal thing in man, / That heeds no call die' -- and the rock strata become, metaphorically at least, the bedrock of insular, genetic inheritance.

But the 'rock' in this novel operates in two other ways. First it acts as a metaphor for the building blocks of genetic inheritance -- the units of germ plasm itself which are communicated from one generation to the next. For example, each of the male heads of the island families or tribes, the Caros, the Bencombs, and the Pierstons, has been involved in the business of quarrying. At the time of the story Pierston's rather shadowy father is still active in the business, and the stone, 'nibbled by his parent from his island rock' (67), is transmitted from father to son who fashions it into works of art -- all carved images of the female form. 'While the son,' Hardy writes, 'had been modelling and chipping his ephemeral fancies into perennial shapes, the father had been persistently chiselling for half a century at the crude original matter of those shapes, the stern, isolated rock in the Channel.' (72) It is as if the stone carries within it racial, genetic, characteristics passed from father to son. They are both carvers of rock, where the business talent of the one is refined into the aesthetic talent of the other: Pierston is literally 'a chip off the old block'. Curiously, no mention is made of Pierston's mother; inheritance in his case comes through the paternal line. In contrast, the inherited characteristics of the three Avices are exclusively maternal while their respective fathers are marginalized and play little or no part in the unfolding drama. Yet here again, genetic transmission is expressed through lapidary metaphor, and when Pierston says of the second Avice that he knows 'the perfect and pure quarry she was dug from' (118), he speaks of his intuitive genetic understanding of her.

Second, the rock substance of the island serves to draw the community together as an emblem of their biological closeness. The material of the buildings they inhabit is dug from the same quarries as Pierston's father's blocks of oolite. The first Avice's cottage, for example, has about it an almost surreal lapidary quality. It 'was all of stone, not only in walls but in window frames, roof, chimneys, fence, stile, pigsty and stable, almost door' (29); and Pierston is touched by the fact that the second Avice lived in 'the very house that had once been his own home' (152) -- the same house within which he intends to take up residence with the third Avice. (178)

In the late 1890s the debate in England about heredity was very prominent. The foundations had been laid by Darwin's work on the descent of man and variation in animals and plants, [14] but it had been joined by scientists and thinkers like Alfred Wallace, August Weismann, Herbert Spencer and William Galton, all of whom were conducting lively discussions about the issues in contemporary journals at the time that Hardy was writing *The Well-Beloved*. Alfred Wallace published extensively on human selection and on the inherited nature of acquired characteristics in the *Fortnightly Review* and Herbert Spencer conducted a spirited exchange with Weismann in the *Contemporary Review*. We know that Hardy read Weismann, [15] but it is the work of Galton which bears most closely upon *The Well-Beloved*. Unlike the more scientifically technical researches of his contemporaries, Galton's methods were comparative and statistical. In his major works, *Hereditary Genius* (1869), *Inquiries into Human Faculty* (1883) and *Natural Inheritance* (1889), for example, he illustrates the principle of what he calls 'Particulate Inheritance' using an example which anticipates Hardy's metaphor of building materials:

Many modern buildings in Italy are historically known to have been built out of the pillaged structures of older days. Here we may observe a column or a lintel serving the same purpose for a second time, and perhaps bearing an inscription that testifies to its origin, while as to the other stones, though the mason may have chipped them here and there, and altered their shapes a little, few, if any, came direct from the quarry. This simile gives a rude though true idea of the exact meaning of Particulate Inheritance, namely that each piece of the new structure is derived from a corresponding piece of some older one, as a lintel was derived from a lintel, a column from a column, a piece of wall from a piece of wall. [16]

But it is Galton's work on what he called 'Composite Portraiture' which so closely resembles one of the most striking aspects of inherited characteristics in Hardy's novel. Throughout the story, the Well-Beloved finds biological embodiment in individual women, and artistic representation in Pierston's statuary, all of whose physical properties are similar though not identical: 'That liquid sparkle of her eye, that lingual music, that turn of the head, how well he knew it all despite the many superficial changes, and how instantly he would recognize it under whatever complexion, contour, accent, height, or carriage that it might choose to masquerade!' (73) All the manifestations of the Well-Beloved possess what Hardy called in his poem 'the family face'. When, for example, Pierston meets the second Avice he is deeply struck by the genetic replication of detailed aspects of her mother's physiognomy: 'Well he knew the arrangement of those white teeth. In the junction of two of the upper ones there was a slight irregularity; no stranger would have noticed it, nor would he, but that he knew of the same mark in her mother's mouth, and looked for it here.' (106) Similarly, Galton was much preoccupied with the nature of family likeness existing independently of individual variations, and he devised a cunning visual method of identifying it called 'Composite Portraiture'. He collected portraits of groups of individuals photographed in the 'same aspect'. [17] He then superimposed these portraits 'like successive leaves of a book' and re-photographed the collection, one by one on, the same sensitive plate. 'The effect of composite portraiture,' he wrote, 'is to bring into evidence all the traits in which there is agreement, and to leave but as a ghost of a trace of individual peculiarities.' Those who see them for the first time, he added, 'can hardly believe but that one dominant face has overpowered the rest, and that they are composites only in name. When, however, the details are examined, this objection disappears.' [18] What Galton took from collective life into the studio, Hardy returned to an 'ideal ... and frankly imaginative' (26) conception of an island community.

Hardy's treatment of inherited characteristics, however, differs in one important respect from almost all those who were writing about heredity at this time. Darwin, Weismann, Spencer, Wallace and Galton, though they treat of the mechanisms of inheritance, have almost nothing to say about that secondary mechanism by which transmission is made possible -- sexual desire. In contrast, The Well-Beloved is dominated by desire in the figure of Venus, the remains of whose temple lie on the island (97), who pursues Pierston remorselessly, as 'Aphrodite, Ashtaroth, Freja or whatever the love-queen of the isle might have been' (139) and with whose image the sculptor is obsessed. (79, 154-5) The sculptor is forever 'posed, puzzled and perplexed by the legerdemain of a creature -- a deity rather; by Aphrodite, as a poet would put it, as I should put it myself in marble.' (53) Ultimately, the novel questions the difficult problem of the relationship between genetics and sexual selection, between the intensely personalized nature of human desire and the impersonal workings of genetic transmission.

One might expect contemporary psychological theory to provide a clue to the problem which Hardy addresses in this novel, so, even in this pre-Freudian period, it comes as something of a surprise to find that the most eminent studies of human psychology -- Herbert Spencer's The Principles of Psychology (1855) and William James's Principles of Psychology (1890) -- are almost silent on the role of sexual selection in normal human behaviour. I say 'normal' because when studies of human sexual behaviour were undertaken they were done so almost exclusively by nineteenth-century alienists and took the form of elaborate analysis of extremes, and perversions. R. von Krafft-Ebing's Psychopathia Sexualis (1886), A. Binet's 'Le fetichisme dans l'amour' (1887), and A. Moll's Die conträre sexualempfindung (1891) offer little insight into the function of sexuality beyond the walls of the clinic. [19]

Only one writer in this period directly questions the relationship between the mechanisms of inheritance and the nature of human desire: Arthur Schopenhauer, whose work Hardy read in 1891. [20] Why is it, he asks, that although the sexual impulse 'is the ultimate goal of all human effort, exerts an adverse influence on the most important events, interrupts the most serious occupations every hour ... and ... demands the sacrifice sometimes of life or health' it has 'hitherto practically been disregarded by philosophers altogether?' [21] In four related essays, 'On Death and its Relation to the Indestructibility of Our Nature', 'The Life of the Species', 'On Heredity' and 'The Metaphysics of the Love of the Sexes', Schopenhauer anticipates a number of Hardy's central preoccupations in *The Well-Beloved*. In the first, he develops the thesis that 'there is something in us which death cannot destroy' [22] and sees in human life a force which acts in an equal and opposite manner to death - - what he calls 'the act of procreation'. [23] In *The Well-Beloved*, Hardy describes the death-defying shift of the spirit of sexual attraction from body to body as 'metempsychosis' (102). Schopenhauer prefers Darwin's term 'palingenesis'. 'These constant new births,' he writes, 'constitute the succession of the life-dreams of a will which in itself is indestructible' and is 'more correctly denoted by the word palingenesis than by metempsychosis.' [24] In the second essay he deals more extensively with the function of procreation, and the way in which sexual desire in man is 'so pre-eminently the chief concern that no other pleasures make up for the deprivation of its satisfaction'. [25] Sexual desire, says Schopenhauer, is a manifestation of the species' 'desire to live' under the guise of particularized and romanticized love. In contrast to the orthodox view of affection, 'the delusive ecstasy which seizes a man at the sight of a woman whose beauty is suited to him, and pictures to him a union with her as the highest good, is just the *sense of the species*, which, recognising the distinctly expressed stamp of the same, desires to perpetuate it with this individual.' [26] In a similar way, Pierston pursues the Caro girls in the somewhat vain hope that each 'individual nature ... would exactly, ideally, supplement his own imperfect one and round with it the perfect whole' (111). 'For all love,' says Schopen-hauer, 'however ethereally it may bear itself, is rooted in the sexual impulses alone, nay, it absolutely is only a more definitely determined, specialised, and indeed in the strictest sense individualised sexual impulse.' 'If,' he continues, 'one considers the important part which the sexual impulse in all its degrees and nuances plays, not only on the stage and in novels, but also in the real world, where next to the love of life, it shows itself the strongest and most powerful of motives,' [27] one is forced to conclude that its function must lie in '*the composition of the next generation*'. [28]

In this way, Schopenhauer gives a cynical reply to the question which Pierston so often poses to himself: why is he obsessed with a certain genetic type at the expense of reason and happiness? 'The pains,' says Schopenhauer, ' with which for his sexual satisfaction a man carefully chooses a woman with definite qualities which appeal to him individually, and strives so eagerly after her that ... he often sacrifices his own happiness in life ... by love affairs which cost him wealth, honour, and life ... [are] all merely in order to serve the species in the most efficient way'. [29] In *The Well-Beloved*, Hardy never quite reaches this point of cynical detachment. Schopenhauer's utilitarian biologism is not Hardy's, and there is little of Hardy in the way in which Schopenhauer reduces sexual attraction to a catalogue of mechanisms for successful reproduction. But, at the end of the novel, Pierston's physical collapse corresponds simulta-neously with his loss of libidinal desire and the disappearance of his aesthetic propensities. He is a man, like Hardy himself, who felt the full power of sexual promptings, who had experienced the full force of the species' 'will to live', but in whom the processes were never consummated and never bore fruit. Schopenhauer's is an objective, cold, and calculated view of the human sexual condition; Hardy's, in the person of Pierston, is a 'frankly subjective', sympathetic view, but amongst writers of this period only these two seem to confront the stressful, paradoxical relationship between personal fulfilment and biological necessitarianism. They may see the problem from different perspectives, but to the question which rings so plangently through *The Well-Beloved* -- why does the nature of sexual desire seem at once so elusive and yet so determinedly fixed upon one generic type? -- Schopenhauer has an answer which is not so far removed from Hardy's. 'Why,' asks Schopenhauer, 'does the lover hang with complete abandonment on the eyes of his chosen one, and is ready to make every sacrifice for her?' His answer is: 'Because it is his immortal part that longs after her; while it is only his mortal part that desires everything else.' 'That vehement or intense longing directed to a particular woman', he concludes, 'is accordingly an immediate pledge of the indestructibility of the kernel of our being, and of its continued existence in the species.' [30] It is, in Hardy's words, 'The eternal thing in man, / That heeds no call to die.'

NOTES

1 Thomas Hardy, *The Well-Beloved*, New Wessex Edition (London: Macmillan, 1975), p. 202. Henceforth all page references to this edition are given in parentheses in the text.

2 Thomas Hardy, *The Life and Work of Thomas Hardy*, ed. Michael Millgate (London: Macmillan, 1984), p. 304.

3 *Ibid.*

4 Hardy, *Life*, p. 303.

5 Hardy, *Life*, p. 304.

6 'The story of a face which goes through three generations or more, would make a fine novel or poem of the passage of Time. The differences in personality to be ignored.' [This idea was to some extent carried out in the novel *The Well-Beloved*, the poem entitled "Heredity", etc.].' Hardy, *Life*, p. 266.

7 'Heredity' in *The Variorum Edition of the Complete Poems of Thomas Hardy*, ed. James Gibson (London: Macmillan, 1976, 1979), no. 363, p. 434.

8 'Gemmules' was Darwin's term which was superseded by August Weismann's theory of 'germ plasm'. See Hans Stubbe, *History of Genetics*, trans. T.R.W. Waters (Cambridge, Mass. 1972), pp. 167-78 passim.

9   Quoted in August Weismann, *Essays Upon Heredity* (Oxford, 1889), p. 5. Hardy read this collection of essays at the end of 1890. See Hardy, *Life*, p. 240.

10 Weismann, *Essays*, p. 33.

11 John Ferguson McLennan, *Studies in Ancient History comprising a reprint of Primitive Marriage*, new edn. (1886), p. 78.

12 John Brand, *Observations on Popular Antiquities Chiefly Illustrating the Origin of our Vulgar Customs, Ceremonies, and Superstitions* (1877 edn.), p. 346.

13 Brand, *Observations*, p. 347.

14 Charles Darwin, *The Variation of Animals and Plants Under Domestication* (1868) and *The Descent of Man* (1871).

15 See note 8.

16 William Galton, *Natural Inheritance* (1889), p. 8.

17 Galton, *Inquiries into Human Faculty* (1883), p. 8.

18 Galton, *Inquiries*, p. 10.

19 One observation common to these works, however, has a bearing upon the novel. Hiram M. Stanley put it most succinctly in his *Studies in the Evolution of Feeling* (New York, 1895) where he claimed that: 'Sexuality is noted strongly among those who professionally cultivate the aesthetic psychosis, as artists, musicians, and poets'. Indeed, he adds, 'many of the very greatest of these have been so carried away by the tender passions as to transgress the conventions and laws on sexual matters.' (p. 296). In *The Well-Beloved*, the author makes it clear on a number of occasions that Pierston 'would not have stood where he did stand in the ranks of an imaginative profession if he had not been at the mercy of every haunting of the fancy that can beset a man. It was in his weakness as a citizen and a national-unit that his strength lay as an artist, and he felt it childish to complain of susceptibilities not only innate but cultivated.' (110).

20 In May 1891 Hardy copied extensive passages from Schopenhauer's *Studies in Pessimism*, trans. T. Baily Saunders (1891). See *The Literary Notebooks of Thomas Hardy*, ed. Lennart A Björk, entries 1782-1800 and notes. Hardy, according to Björk, also possessed Schopenhauer's *Two Essays*, trans. Madam Karl Hillebrand (1889). See note for entry 1232. We cannot be absolutely sure that he read *The World as Will and Idea*, which appeared in English in 1883, but his interest in the philosopher's works while composing *The Well-Beloved* which first appeared in the *Illustrated London News* in 1892, suggests familiarity.

21 Arthur Schopenhauer, *The World as Will and Idea*, trans. R. B. Haldane and J. Kemp, 3rd edn. (1896), iii, 339 and 338. First translated 1883.

22 *Ibid*, iii, 284.

23 *Ibid*, iii, 292.

24 *Ibid*, iii, 300.

25 *Ibid*, iii, 313.

26 *Ibid*, iii, 347.

27 *Ibid*, iii, 339.

28 *Ibid*, iii, 340.

29 *Ibid*, iii, 347-8.

30 *Ibid*, iii, 373.

Hardy Among the Moderns

R.P. Draper

In 1980 Samuel Hynes published an important essay, 'The Hardy Tradition in Modern English Poetry' [1], in which he argued that, notwithstanding T.S. Eliot's celebrated emphasis on the significance of 'tradition' (as in his essay on 'Tradition and the Individual Talent') the modernist movement in poetry was in fact a departure from literary tradition -- taking 'tradition' in its proper sense of 'handing down a set of values and a way of writing which maintain continuity between the present and the past'. Hardy, on the other hand, could well be regarded as truly traditional, and it could be argued that his followers (Hynes cites as examples Robert Frost, Edward Thomas, the early Lawrence, Edmund Blunden, Robert Graves, Andrew Young, C. Day Lewis, Geoffrey Grigson and Philip Larkin) show their allegiance to him, not by slavish imitation, but by upholding recognisably the same features and principles in their verse. What these are is neatly encapsulated by Hynes in his 'summary definition' of 'the Hardy tradition':

...it is English and primarily concerned with actual nature and with man's relation to it; it is physical, not transcendental, but it is nevertheless religious in the sense that its nature is not 'neutralized'; it is descriptive rather than metaphorical or symbolic; it is rooted in time, but not in history; it is often concerned with the reality of memory, and so is retrospective, sometimes regretful and melancholy, but also ironic and stoic; it observes the world, not the self. Formally, the tradition is conservative, but inventive...The verse is never free, the syntax is never fragmented, the sense is never in doubt -- difficult, yes, but not doubtful. [2]

This view has been interestingly developed and modified by John Powell Ward who dovetails Hardy into a distinctively English line extending from Wordsworth to Larkin. The 'regretful' and 'melancholy' elements in Hynes' definition receive particular emphasis in Ward's line, and he adds a slightly paradoxical strain of the 'unpoetic' which involves almost a mistrust of the poet's basic tool of language. Deriving from a 'strongly Protestant and perhaps Puritan inheritance' with its 'suspicion of the luxurious or guiltless, or even the confident' this is a line of poetry in which 'words are enjoyed, not for their own sakes as palpable and richly semantic media, but as embodying the rhythm and shape that seem to manage and ease the very pain they try to express.' [3]

Ward is concerned with something which is at once wider and narrower than Hynes: wider in that it includes a tradition of English poetry which extends from the end of the eighteenth century right through to the present day, and narrower in that it focuses on a melancholy strain which in Hynes' definition is only one element among several in the Hardy tradition. Both critics agree, however, in stressing the conservative nature of the writing which constitutes their respective traditions; and both suggest, or imply, that modernist experiment is alien to Hardy. To some extent this is true. As Hynes observes, 'The verse is never free, the syntax is never fragmented.' On the face of it nothing in Hardy's *Complete Poems* is comparable in form with Eliot's *The Waste Land* or Pound's *Cantos*; nothing resembles the discordancies of Macdiarmid's *A Drunk Man Looks at the Thistle*, or the teasing elegancies of Wallace Stevens' 'The Man with the Blue Guitar', or the colloquial freedom and seemingly random collocations of William Carlos Williams'*Paterson.* Yet there are points of contact. Hardy is also innovative and deeply interested in the relationship between his poetic forms and the distinctively late-nineteenth-century/early twentieth-century vision, or undermining of vision, which they communicate. though certainly not an ideological moder*nist*, he is emphatically a self-aware modern; and despite the obvious differences between his work, situated as it is in a national tradition, and that of the more internationally minded modernists with their accent on a paradoxically anti-traditional tradition, there are features both of form and content which make that work recognisably modern.

Certain of Hardy's critical pronouncements, scattered and unsystematic though they are, reveal him as sympathetic to art that is exploratory and experimental rather than merely a continuance of the established. In a comment recorded in the *Life* dated 5 August 1890 he rejects the conventional idea that realism is art and offers a definition of art as 'a changing of the actual proportions and order of things, so as to bring out more forcibly than might otherwise be done that feature in them which appeals most strongly to the idiosyncrasy of the artist.' And there is a record of a remark made three years earlier preferring the paintings of 'the much decried, mad, late-Turner' to those of Richard Parkes Bonington (even though he had a landscape attributed to the latter in his drawing room at Max Gate) on the grounds that he is no longer interested in 'scenic paintings', but wants 'to see the deeper reality underlying the scenic, the expression of what are sometimes called abstract imaginings.' [4] This is in accord with Hardy's approval of 'someone of insight' who perceived the later Verdi as a kind of phoenix arising from the ashes of his popularity as the composer of *Il Trovatore* [5]; and the demand for something more radical than surface romanticism recalls the famous description of Egdon Heath in *The Return of the Native*, in particular the suggestion that traditional Mediterranean standards of beauty are played out, modern men perhaps finding themselves 'in closer and closer harmony with external things wearing a sombreness distasteful to our race when it was young.' [6]

Closer to Hardy's own practice as a poet are the comments made, in response to critics who slighted *Wessex Poems* (his first volume of verse, published in 1899), on the relation between poetry and Gothic architecture:

In the reception of this and later volumes of Hardy's poems there was, he said, as regards form, the inevitable ascription to ignorance of what was really choice after full knowledge. That the author loved the art of concealing art was undiscerned. For instance, as to rhythm. Years earlier he had decided that too regular a beat was bad art. He had fortified himself in his opinion by thinking of the analogy of architecture, between which art and that of poetry he had discovered, to use his own words, that there existed a close and curious parallel, both arts, unlike some others, having to carry a rational content inside their artistic form. He knew that in architecture cunning irregularity is of enormous worth, and it is obvious that he carried on into his verse, perhaps in part unconsciously, the Gothic art-principle in which he had been trained -- the principle of spontaneity, found in mouldings, tracery, and such like -- resulting in the 'unforeseen' (as it has been called) character of his metres and stanzas, that of stress rather than of syllable, poetic texture rather than poetic veneer; the latter kind of thing, under the name of 'constructed ornament', being what he, in common with every Gothic student, had been taught to avoid as the plague. He shaped his poetry accordingly, introducing metrical pauses, and reversed beats; and found for his trouble that some particular line of a poem exemplifying this principle was greeted with a would-be jocular remark that such a line 'did not make for immortality'. The same critic might have gone to one of our cathedrals (to follow up the analogy of architecture), and on discovering that the carved leafage of some capital or spandrel in the best period of Gothic art strayed freakishly out of its bounds over the moulding, where by rule it had no business to be, or that the enrichments of a string-course were not accurately spaced; or that there was a sudden blank in a wall where a window was to be expected from formal measurement, have declared with equally merry conviction, 'This does not make for immortality'. [7]

Dennis Taylor has shown how this passage relates to Victorian speculation on prosody, in a tradition stemming from Hegel, and running via Ruskin, Coventry Patmore, R.L. Stevenson, Robert Bridges, and others to a little-known article by Ramsay Traquair on 'Free Verse and the Parthenon' (published in 1919) which Hardy admired, and by which, Taylor suggests, he was probably influenced. [8] Here, interestingly enough, a connection is being established which reaches both backwards and forwards. Hardy's analogy with Gothic architecture serves not only to justify incidental departures from a prosodic norm, but also to create a context in which twentieth-century free verse may be considered. In this respect he may be compared with Gerard Manley Hopkins who similarly provides an important bridging of the gap between Victorian and modern via his speculations on 'sprung rhythm'; and with D.H. Lawrence whose remarks to Edward Marsh defending his early verse on the grounds that it should be read by 'length' rather than 'stress' ('as a matter of movements in space than footsteps hitting the earth') can be seen as a prelude to the sensitively controlled irregularity he allows himself in the later poems of *Birds, Beasts and Flowers* and *Last Poems*. [9] This in turn can be related backwards to the free verse of Walt Whitman's *Leaves of Grass* and forwards to the 'new measure' evolved by William Carlos Williams [10] and its profound influence on modern American poets such as the Black Mountain school and women poets such as Adrienne Rich and Denise Levertov.

For Hardy, of course, the 'rational content' inside the artistic form of either architecture or poetry remains fundamental, and corresponding to this is the metrical discipline he continues to submit to even when he allows himself considerable liberty with the 'unforeseen' resulting from 'the principle of spontaneity'. The consequence is that he can sound simultaneously traditional and modern. A good example is 'In Tenebris II', where the theme especially lends itself to an ironic criss-cross of the mock-modestly old-fashioned, the contemporary with-it (i.e. reflecting contemporary attitudes of the 1890s -- the poem is dated 1895-6), and a subdued foreshadowing of less uncritical attitudes. Although its seven-stressed line, related to the old 'fourteener', is an ancient metre and moves with a ponderous, shambling gait, the prose accents of the spoken voice are superimposed on it in such a way as to create a counterpoint between the old and the new. Slight, but significant, readjustments of emphasis are constantly forced on the reader, especially with regard to the use of possessive pronouns. In line 3, for example, 'And my eyes have not the vision in them to discern what to these is so clear', a slightly sardonic counter-metrical emphasis falls on 'my', which in its turn points up the half-hidden satirical pun on 'vision'. Similarly, in line 9, 'Their dawns bring lusty joys, it seems; their evenings all that is sweet', the sly accent on 'Their', coupled with what might easily be dismissed as the prosaically superfluous 'it seems', gives an ironic tinge to what follows. The varied rhythms capturing the movement of actual speech also give the lines an astonishingly dramatic flexibility, heightening the effect of spontaneity. The shouts of 'the many and strong' that 'All's well with us: ruers have nought to rue!', coupled with the bustling, self-confident movement of 'Breezily go they, breezily come; their dust smokes around their career', contrast tellingly with the subdued and diffident accents in which the 'I' persona speaks. (This persona is perhaps Hardy himself, but if so, Hardy adopting a certain stance of antithetical modesty which forms an ironic counter-balance to the brashness of his majority figures.) He seems to accept himself as a superfluous outsider, 'one better he were not here', and in the last stanza that alienation poses rhetorically as a kind of public dismissal. But the charac-terisation of the persona to be dismissed turns into a condemnation of the majority 'clash' through subordinate clauses which have yet another kind of movement, more sensitively feeling its way, and requiring a more thoughtfully discriminating response from the reader:

Who holds that if way to the Better there be, it exacts a full look at the Worst,

Who feels that delight is a delicate growth cramped by crookedness, custom, and fear.

The result is to compel a revision of the notion of misshaping implicit in the 'one shaped awry' of the last line, and to turn the tables on the kind of order implicit in the final 'he disturbs the order here'.

F.R. Leavis, among others, has noted the powerful effect achieved by the change of key in the last stanza of 'The Voice'; after the plangent urgency of 'Woman much missed, how you call to me, call to me' comes the onomatopoeically 'faltering'

Thus I; faltering forward,
  Leaves around me falling,
Wind oozing thin through the thorn from norward,
  And the woman calling.

Enchantment and disenchantment are part of the emotional dialectic that goes on in much of Hardy's love poetry, and a shift from lyric to prosaic is a not uncommon way of signalling it. One is reminded of Eliot's adaptations of bathos in 'Prufrock' or *The Waste Land*, except that Hardy rarely employs the figure in order to sound 'jug jug to dirty ears'. He has more in common with the W. H. Auden of 'Lay your sleeping head, my love, / Human on my faithless arm', or the Philip Larkin of 'Love Songs in Age' with its 'glare of that much-mentioned brilliance, love' which promises 'to solve, and satisfy', but 'had not done so then, and could not now'. That is to say, he shares their modern sense of promise and disappointment as equally valid rather than successively cancelling experiences, and, like them, he creates a poetic texture which is correspondingly multi-faceted -- designedly uneven in movement and diction.

In this sense 'Channel Firing' and 'The Convergence of the Twain' may be regarded as quintessentially modern poems. They are complementary to each other, the first representing Hardy in his comic, the second in his tragic mood, but neither is tonally exclusive. On the contrary, each is penetrated in a very modern manner by elements which belong to the mood of the other so that to call either 'comic' or 'tragic' seems a misleading simplification.

'Channel Firing' is a masterpiece of the Bakhtinian 'carnivalesque' -- a confusion of genres much admired by modern literary theorists. Raman Selden's characterisation of this kind of writing as one in which 'opposites are mingled...the sacred is profaned... Everything authoritative, rigid or serious is subverted, loosened and mocked' is nicely applicable to 'Channel Firing', as is his suggestion that carnival promotes the idea of texts as 'multi-levelled and resistant to unification.' [11] The variety of voices in 'Channel Firing' is still more marked than in 'In Tenebris II'. There is the 'one' who doubts the sanity of the world and its capacity to improve; there is the voice of Parson Thirdly

93

who regrets his forty years of preaching and wishes he had 'stuck to pipes and beer'; and there is the narrator himself speaking, when he uses the collective 'we', as a member of the company of the dead, and, in the second and last stanzas, as the poetically evocative commentator on the scene. To some extent these are typical Hardy figures, part of a rural chorus such as one finds in the novels, and, more particularly, in other poems like 'Voices from Things Growing in a Churchyard' or 'Friends Beyond' where it is also the dead who speak. Their remarks are commonplace enough, but defamiliarised and made more telling by the bizarre context of the booming disturbance which causes them to sit upright in their graves.

More startling still is the bluff, scolding voice Hardy gives to his 'God', who profanes the sacred and subverts the rigid or serious with a disconcertingly carnivalesque verve. Colloquial down-to-earthness, jostling with the archaic-sounding 'Christes' and the clattering feminine rhyme in

> Mad as hatters
> They do no more for Christes sake
> Than you who are helpless in such matters

creates a comic (but not unattractive) image of the deity, which climaxes in the resonant mockery of

> 'Ha, ha. It will be warmer when
> I blow the trumpet...'

This is a conscious (and in another author might seem deliberately modernist) adaptation of the Book of Job, 39, 24-5, where the Lord speaks to Job of the valour of the warhorse: 'He swalloweth the ground with fierceness and rage: neither believeth he that it is the sound of the trumpet. He saith among the trumpets, Ha, ha; and he smelleth the battle afar off, the thunder of the captains, and the shouting.' God and the Royal Navy are alike deliberately travestied by this allusion, as is the conventional idea of the Judgement Day. And still more effective is the sudden suspension of this comically transformed image of the *dies irae* when God relaxes into a parenthesis which aborts all his previous performance:

> '...(if indeed
> I ever do; for you are men,
> And rest eternal sorely need).'

On another plane are the words which evoke, not the biblical warhorse, but the non-human creatures of the real world:

94

While drearisome
 Arose the howl of wakened hounds:
The mouse let fall the altar-crumb,
 The worms drew back into the mounds,
 The glebe cow drooled

along with those which form a curiously potent coda to the whole poem:

Again the guns disturbed the hour,
Roaring their readiness to avenge,
As far inland as Stourton Tower,
And Camelot, and starlit Stonehenge.

Such lines employ registers which are different again from those of the rest of the poem. The dogs, mouse, worms and cattle evoked in brief detail with oddly distinctive diction and rhythms (especially 'The glebe cow drooled') command a quite un-satirical respect, while the designedly stagey rhetoric of 'Roaring their readiness to revenge' in the final stanza is sandwiched between its preceding line, where 'disturbed' has a soberingly critical force (it has something in common with the 'disturbs' at the end of 'In Tenebris II'), and the strangely remote glamour of the last two lines. These curious oscillations confirm the impression that the poem as a whole is not an organic unity, but a succession of deliberately contrived discordancies. In its comically unsettling, disconcerting way it works, and yet exactly how it works, and to what effect, are themselves curiously disturbing questions.

'The Convergence of the Twain' has greater unity of tone that 'Channel Firing' -- a unity which it is easier to label 'tragic', and to that extent it is perhaps less amenable to modern and post-modern critical ideas. Nevertheless, with its bizarre linguistic juxtapositions and its disruption of normal narrative sequence it is equally effective in undermining formal expectations. Hardy's fondness for lexical oddities such as 'stilly couches she', 'currents thrid', 'slimed', 'Lie lightless', and the coupling of impressively polysyllabic with plainer, monosyllabic words ('salamandrine fires', '"What does this vaingloriousness down here?"', 'far and dissociate', 'consummation comes, and jars two hemispheres') is a powerful reinforcement of the weird *mise en scené* he creates -- a luxury liner, the ultimate expression of 'human vanity, / And the Pride of Life that planned her', lying on the ocean-floor as anomalous intruder in a totally other world of 'sea-worm' and 'Dim moon-eyed fishes'. These are distinctively modern discordancies. That the poem also offers in its second half (from stanzas VI to XI) a 'rational' explanation, like Tom Stoppard unfolding his bizarre juxtapositions in *Jumpers* or *After Magritte,* is in keeping with the 'rational content' which Hardy still deemed necessary to his Gothic art; but the dominant impression remains one of a marked disproportioning which 'appeals most strongly to the idiosyncracy of the artist', and which highlights the irrational 'jarring' of 'two hemispheres'.

Hardy's handling of the stanza, particularly in 'The Convergence of the Twain', is another means by which he subverts his own rational content. The structure is firm and clear: two six-syllabled, three-stressed lines are balanced by one twelve-syllabled, six-stressed line, and the whole is bound together by a simple AAA rhyme-scheme. However, rhythmical and syllabic irregularities vary this structure, and, especially after stanza V, as the narrative element in the poem gets under way a largely static, end-stopped stanza gives way to one which rides over its own divisions with enjambements. The result is some conflict between the run-on demanded by prose sense and the isolation of words and phrases created by the pattern of the stanza. For example, 'mate' at the end of VII, line 1, is part of the run-on of prose sense from VI to VII in which the Immanent Will is seen as preparing a sinister husband for the 'Titanic' even while the latter is being built. This development of the standard convention by which a ship is treated as of female gender is itself part of a process of renewal of dead metaphor and gives the maritime disaster the added, if shadowy, dimension of marital conflict which is particularly searing in the context of what we now know of Hardy's own domestic circumstances in 1912 (the year of the sinking of the Titanic) and the great elegiac poems written after the death of Emma. In addition, however, the isolation of the word 'mate' allows at least the momentary possibility of its being read as 'checkmate', with the suggestion of a game of chess lurking in the background, and of a coldly inhuman intellectual design in contrast with the very real human emotion surrounding the loss of the great liner.

Other examples of renewal or enrichment of meaning through enjambement and stanzaic isolation of words are to be found in poems such as 'A Two Years' Idyll', where in lines 21-3 --

> Nothing came after: romance straight forsook
> Quickly somehow
> Life when we sped from our nook,

the separation of the phrase 'Quickly somehow' from the rest of its clause makes its otherwise banal language more meaningful; 'Without Ceremony', where the enjambement of 'career / Off' in 'And when you'd a mind to career / Off anywhere' (lines 6-7) gives an oddly disturbing prominence to Emma's unpredictability (or what seemed such to Hardy at the time); and 'In Front of the Landscape', lines 21-3, --

> Some as with slow-born tears that brinily trundled
> Over the wrecked
> Cheeks that were fair in their flush-time, ash now with anguish,

where, besides foregrounding the peculiarity of the phrase 'brinily trundled' and the alliterated contrast between young and old cheeks, the disjoining of 'Over' and 'wrecked' from the verb and noun which they respectively modify again disinters a half-buried metaphor of shipwreck.

These are all instances of the 'Gothic' procedures by which Hardy, while retaining the support of rational discourse, can also, whether consciously or not, break down the tendency of syntax to subordinate the meaningfulness of individual words and phrases, especially those usually regarded as unimportant grammatical connectives, to an overall paraphraseable prose sense. Hardy's debt here is to Browning, but he is also a major contributor to the development of enjambed versification which becomes an important feature of modern poetry, with exemplars in William Carlos Williams, Robert Lowell, E.E. Cummings, Richard Wilbur and Philip Larkin.

As Stephen Cushman has shown, William Carlos Williams' experiments with metric led him to the discovery of 'the straddled leg' of enjambement, and in a brilliant series of analyses Cushman shows how expressively redemptive of language this can be. [12] Hardy reached a similar goal by what may have been a similar route -- his interest in metrical variation. Breaking down the monotony of the foot leads naturally to breaking down the monotony of the line, and the complementary next step is the overriding of both the line and the stanza by enjambement. Although Hardy does not make such frequent use of it as Williams and Cummings (the inventive master of a great many varieties of stanzaic form, he normally contains his enjambement within the stanzaic structure) his work reveals that he knows how to avoid the predictability of the end-stopped stanza as well as that of the end-stopped line. Examples include the transition from the first to the second stanza of 'At Castle Boterel'; the prolonging of the catalogue of unheeded weather features through stanzas 3-5 of 'She Hears the Storm'; and, most strikingly, the opening of 'The Re-Enactment':

Between the folding sea-downs,
    In the gloom
Of a wailful wintry nightfall,
    When the boom
Of the ocean, like a hammering in a hollow tomb,

Throbbed up the copse-clothed valley
    From the shore
To the chamber where I darkled,
    Sunk and sore
With gray ponderings why my Loved one had not come before

To salute me in the dwelling
    That of late
I had hired to waste a while in --
    Dim of date,
Quaint, and remote -- wherein I now expectant sate;

On the solitude, unsignalled,
    Broke a man
Who, in air as if at home there,

      Seemed to scan
Every fire-flecked nook of the apartment span by span.

   Here the suspended syntax creates an expectant forward movement matching
the expectancy of the 'darkled' I' of the poem, but its baffled and retarded
progress through the intricacies and enjambements of four stanzas also creates
a powerful sense of the growing frustration and disappointment of the 'I'. The
technique is built upon -- and used even more effectively -- by Larkin in a poem
like 'The Building':

      see, as they climb
To their appointed levels, how their eyes
Go to each other, guessing; on the way

Someone's wheeled past, in washed-to-rags ward clothes:
They see him, too. They're quiet. To realise
This new thing held in common makes them quiet,
For past these doors are rooms, and rooms past those,
And more rooms yet, each one further off

And harder to return from; and who knows
Which he will see, and when?

The prose sense cutting across the stanza structure creates a simultaneous
awareness of order and disorder which is just as disturbing as the more overt
disruptions and ellipses of self-consciously modernist verse. Both Hardy and
Larkin create a new disquiet without abandoning the traditional.

   But perhaps the feature which links Hardy most obviously with developments
taking place in modern verse is the clear, firm concreteness of his imagery, and
the focus in so many of his poems on what is seen and heard as the substance
from which meaning is distilled rather than allegorised. This suggests a connection with the Imagists, even though Hardy was never one of them. His virtues
were recognised by Pound, and certainly poems like 'Overlooking the River
Stour' and 'On the Esplanade' have as much Imagist hardness and clarity, if
they are not quite so laconic, as Pound, Hulme or H.D.. Significantly, however,
Hardy's strategy, compared with theirs, is a negative one -- to make the unseen,
unheard have greater effect than the seen and heard. While the moon image
in 'On the Esplanade':

The broad bald moon edged up where the sea was wide,
   Mild, mellow-faced

suggests that of Hulme's 'Autumn':

> I walked abroad
> And saw the ruddy moon lean over a hedge
> Like a red-faced farmer

(there is some kinship even in the humorous effect, though Hardy is less blatant than Hulme), the development of Hardy's lines is towards 'A lady unseen', and his conclusion is of a very un-Imagist kind:

> Yea, such did I mark. That, behind,
> My Fate's masked face crept near me I did not know!

Again, in 'Overlooking the River Stour' still more brilliantly descriptive Imagist details (for example, 'The swallows flew in the curves of an eight / ...Like little crossbows animate' and 'Planing up shavings of spray / A moor-hen darted out') are finally devalued, with a harrowing, though unspecified, tragic significance, as 'less things' compared with the neglected 'more behind my back'.

What makes Hardy an imagist (with a small rather than a capital 'i') is his intense interest in the actual. The specificity of his poetry is the metonymic specificity of a novelist (again, to do him justice, as noted by Pound). What Marjorie Perloff says of Robert Lowell -- that he is 'confessional' by virtue of the realist-seeming detail (sometimes autobiographically reliable, sometimes not) and the *air* of immediacy he infuses into his poetry [13], could also be said of Hardy. And over and above that, the actual for him is the actuality of a region, which makes him the most important precursor not only of regional novelists like Faulkner and the early Lawrence, but also of regional poets like R.S. Thomas and Seamus Heaney, for whom the local, as with Hardy, is the universal.

For Hardy, however, the actual is ultimately only of importance in so far as it is stamped with the impress of the human. The same goes for history and tradition:

> Primaeval rocks form the road's steep border,
>   And much have they faced there, first and last,
> Of the transitory in Earth's long order;
>
> But what they record in colour and cast
>   Is -- that we two passed. [14]

The kind of literary/historical/cultural freight carried by T. S. Eliot in *The Waste Land* or Pound in his *Cantos* is quite untypical of Hardy. When he does consciously interact with other texts it is the human context which remains to the fore. This is true even when oblivion of the human seems to be the theme. For example, in 'Drawing Details in an Old Church' specificity of sound in connection with the church-bell's tolling ('I hear the bell-rope sawing, / And the oil-less axle grind') is combined with literary allusion ('I ask not whom it tolls for'), but Donne's 'it tolls for thee' is apparently replaced by indifference. The 'I' of the poem is prompted to imagine a stranger in a similar situation hearing, yet being incurious of, the funeral knell for the speaker himself. Yet this seeming negation of human uniqueness has the paradoxical effect of giving poignant emphasis to it; the bell does toll for thee, if in a totally different way from that envisaged by Donne. Similarly (though the technique in this instance is admittedly rather more heavy-handed) the allusion to the deaths of Tom and Maggie in *The Mill on the Floss* implied by the title of the poem 'In Death Divided', while rejecting the sentimental comfort of George Eliot's '*not* divided', relentlessly focuses the painful truth of the actual human situation. In neither example of intertextuality is it the literary tradition as such which is given emphasis, but the human reality denuded of a no longer credible consolation.

Typically, then, Hardy has points of contact with the moderns -- enough for him to be reckoned as one of them, as he was indeed their contemporary, and even beyond that, to be recognised as the precursor of later modernist and post-modern developments. Which is not to deny that he also has much in common with the Victorians and the poets of the late nineteenth century, as he was also *their* contemporary. Yet, unlike Yeats, he did not have a career which showed a striking change from nineteenth-century to modern -- a casting aside of embroidered mythologies in favour of the greater enterprise of walking naked. What he does share, however, with Yeats is continuance of belief in rational content and a poetic practice which maintains contact with, even while modifying, the discursive, grammatical and metric structures of his predecessors. The sense of 'traditional' appropriate to him is one which involves continuity with the past, but adaptation to the present, and also alertness to the future. It leaves a Hardy who is firmly and distinctively his own self, but not an alien figure among his contemporaries -- one who had no interest in establishing a movement, or joining a faction, and certainly not one who would presume, Pound-like, to tell other writers what they should do, yet for all that one whom both his contemporaries and successors could respect, and by whose example they could, and did, learn, without becoming either imitators or disciples. If few of them can be said to be sealed of the tribe of Hardy (exception must be made for C. Day Lewis and Philip Larkin, who more or less claimed this distinction for themselves), they recognised a distinguished fellow-poet who moved among them as, in his own discreetly inimitable way, a quite formidable modern Master.

NOTES

1 In *Thomas Hardy: The Writer and His Background*, edited by Norman Page, Bell & Hyman, London, 1980, pp. 173-91.

2 *Ibid.*, p. 189.

3 John Powell Ward, *The English Line: Poetry of the Unpoetic from Wordsworth to Larkin.* (Macmillan, Basingstoke & London, 1991), pp. 10-11.

4 *The Life of Thomas Hardy, 1840-1928* [attributed to Florence Emily Hardy, but effectively the work of Hardy himself]. (Macmillan, Basingstoke & London, 1962), reprinted 1972, pp. 228 and 185.

5 *Ibid.*, p. 300.

6 *The Return of the Native.* New Wessex edition (hb), (Macmillan, Basingstoke & London, 1975), p. 34.

7 *Ibid.*, pp. 300-1.

8 See Dennis Taylor, *Hardy's Metres and Victorian Prosody.* (Oxford University Press, Oxford, 1988), pp. 27-48.

9 Letter to Edward Marsh, 18 November 1913. *The Letters of D.H. Lawrence*, Vol. II, edited by George J. Zytaruk and James T. Boulton, (Cambridge University Press, Cambridge, 1981), pp. 102-05. For Lawrence's views on free verse see his Introduction to the American edition of *New Poems* (1920), reprinted in *The Complete Poems of D.H. Lawrence*, edited by Vivian de Sola Pinto and warren Roberts., (Heinemann, London, 1964) (reprinted 1967), Vol. I, pp. 181-6.

10 Letter from William Carlos Williams to Richard Eberhart, May 23, 1954. Reprinted in *Modern Poets on Modern Poetry*, edited by James Scully, (McGraw Hill Inc., New York, 1965),(Fontana/Collins, London, 1966), pp. 71-2.

11 Raman Selden: *A Reader's Guide to Contemporary Literary Theory*, (Harvester Press, Brighton, 1985), pp. 18-19.

12 Stephen Cushman, *William Carlos Williams and the Meanings of Measure.* (Yale University Press, New Haven & London, 1985), p. 15.

13 See Marjorie G. Perloff: *The Poetic Art of Robert Lowell*, (Cornell University Press, Ithaca & London, 1973), pp. 87-8.

14 'At Castle Boterel', lines 21-5.

Third Floor, Hotel Rex, The Esplanade, Weymouth
Looking out over the bay at 5 a.m.

Clean daylight hurts. A smell of air.

A throbbing tractor grinds back and forth,
Stolidly clearing litter and bottles.
The waves so tiny; barely more
Than cream that shifts when a cat laps.
So magic a time. Do I wake or sleep?

A laze of shops around the curve.
A church spire rockets above its reflection.

Empty cleaned sand. The gulls bewail
A life so clean: a mirror-world
Science-fiction dreams, yet never comes;
Bar now; right now; where sea meets sand.

The harbour's masted flatness filming
The street-lamps' equally tiny heights.
A kids' stopped train, a stilled Big Wheel.
The neat hotels like postage stamps.
A man with backpack stoops and strides.

The gulls besiege. In my third-floor room
I feel like a weightless astronaut,
And lean and hang out over a world
Left by unknown inhabitants.

Where late one day on the esplanade
A known old man forewent his love.

Loss and Gain

Just reading this thing about
Jude the Obscure and those
Judgements Thomas Hardy bore.
July 1895: a bishop burns a copy!

Autumn 1992. The earth is earth in
Arafat and Boston and Cerne
Abbas. There are wonderful people.
Afternoon. Apple-picking time.

The Cathedral Church of Christ

Tourists, the odd cleric
Swept like a handful of sand
By the skunk wind under its doors.

The name of Canterbury
The name of Canterbury

At night I ascend the hill
North of the town. There she is,
Riding her lights, at anchor,
Foghorning to England to reboard and sail.

JOHN POWELL WARD

Hardy Inscribed
Dennis Taylor

There are many reasons for Thomas Hardy's fascination with the printed page. In childhood, the printed page was his gateway to a world of dreams, knowledge, and romance. In young adulthood, it became a ticket out of the world of architectural labour and into the world of literature. It eventually became his passage to fame and fortune, and the alternative to social and mortal anonymity. It promised, in his own case at least, to overcome the class system, the need to labour and be exhausted, and even the need to die.

To be written or printed on a page, or to be inscribed in any fashion, was to be preserved. In his early 'Ditty', Hardy sings:

> Upon that fabric fair
>   'Here is she!'
> Seems written everywhere
>   Unto me.

Immortal justice depends on the hope that 'Heaven inscrolls the wrong' ('A Sign-Seeker'), and that wrongs are 'Written indelibly' on God's mind ('By the Earth's Corpse'). The alternative to being so inscribed is being unremembered, a horror which Gray attributes to the obscure as well as the rich in his 'Elegy'. For Hardy, the equivalent of being unremembered is not surviving in an inscription. Thus the alternative to the printed page or inscribed memorial is the 'levelled churchyard' in which all is lost. In his copy of Jeremy Taylor's *Holy Living and Dying* (London, 1850, Colby College collection), Hardy underlined Taylor's description of death as 'the land where all things are forgotten' (p. 389). About those who fought the Roman legions, Hardy wrote in *A Tryst at an Ancient Earthwork*: 'not a page, not a stone, has preserved their fame'. Not having something inscribed, printed, defined, traced, is to be vulnerable to unseen forces of decay and destruction: 'There is some hid dread afoot / That we cannot trace' ('A January Night'). [1]

The printed name or description is a form of permanence, but one that takes on an odd independence. The printed form is an externalized, objectified form of personality and intelligence, and the form is oddly indifferent to the existence of the person inscribed. In *Desperate Remedies*, Cytherea advertises as a governess, and then she sees the printed advertisement (chapter 2, part 1):

A YOUNG LADY is desirous of meeting with an ENGAGEMENT AS
GOVERNESS OR COMPANION

Hardy writes:

> It seemed a more material existence than her own that she
> saw thus delineated on the paper.'That can't be myself; how
> odd I look!' she said, and smiled.

In some poems Hardy makes play with the oddity of seeing a printed name but
not knowing its meaning until later or too late:

> I read your name when you were strange to me,
> Where it stood blazoned bold with many more;
> I passed it vacantly, and did not see
> Any great glory in the shape it wore.
>
> O cruelty, the insight barred me then!
> ('To an Actress', 190)

Or, in reverse, the printed page which was once alive with life loses its
meaningfulness:

> But from the letters of her name
> The radiance has waned away!
> ('Her Initials', 11)

Print is such a powerful image for Hardy that it not only records but replaces
the living person. The face for example is sometimes described as a page of print,
needing to be read, as in *The Return of the Native*. About Clym, Hardy writes
(III, chapter 1):

> The observer's eye was arrested, not by his face as a picture, but by his face
> as a page; not by what it was, but by what it recorded. His features were at-
> tractive in the light of symbols, as sounds intrinsically common become at-
> tractive in language, and as shapes intrinsically simple become interesting
> in writing.

Johnny Nunsuch looks at Mrs. Yeobright (IV, chapter 6):

He gazed into her face in a vague, wondering manner, like that of one examining some strange old manuscript the key to whose characters is undiscoverable.

In *The Mayor of Casterbridge*, chapter 16, Hardy writes of Farfrae:

The young man...could now read the lines and the folds of Henchard's strongly-traced face as if they were clear verbal inscriptions.

These passages may have a source in Charlotte Brontë's *The Professor* (chapter 2):

I showed him my countenance with the confidence that one would show an unlearned man a letter written in Greek; he might see lines, and trace characters, but he could make nothing of them; my nature was not his nature, and its signs were to him like the words of an unknown tongue.

Sometimes these facial inscriptions are clear transcriptions of the person. Sometimes they are opaque, with the real person hidden behind them. Faces are like printed inscriptions, sometimes understood, sometimes not.

In the novels, not only a face but an entire life's story is likened to a piece of writing or print briefly seen. In *The Mayor of Casterbridge*, chapter 25, Hardy writes of Elizabeth-Jane:

She stoically looked from her bedroom window, and contemplated her fate as if it were written on the top of the church-tower hard by.

In *Jude the Obscure*, I, chapter 6, Hardy describes Jude's reaction to Arabella:

It had been no vestal who chose *that* missile for opening her attack on him. He saw this with his intellectual eye, just for a short fleeting while, as by the light of a falling lamp one might momentarily see an inscription on a wall before being enshrouded in darkness.

About the deaths of Eustacia and Wildeve, Hardy writes in *The Return of the Native* (VI, chapter 1):

Misfortune had struck them gracefully, cutting off their erratic histories with a catastrophic dash.

Here Hardy interprets the idea of fate, 'fatum', something said by the gods, something written in the stars, with a strange literalness, as thought it were an imprinted page.

The life story imaged as a printed page is not only what has happened but what might happen. Eustacia is tempted by the pistols (V, chapter 4):

Eustacia regarded them long, as if they were the page of a book in which she read a new and a strange matter.

Interestingly, *The Return of the Native* contains the most examples of this technique of using in astonishingly literal ways the image of peering at a line of print or at an inscription. Another evocative example is when Venn, the reddleman, once more reads Thomasin's rejection letter (I, chapter 9).

The writing had originally been traced on white paper, but the letter had now assumed a pale red tinge from the accident of its situation; and the black strokes of writing thereon looked like the twigs of a winter hedge against a vermilion sunset.

Venn's letter, with its black strokes of writing, is a sign of intelligence but, as a physical sign, subject to change. As it is seen in different circumstances and affected by different physical conditions, it changes its physical character while continuing to inscribe an old intelligibility.

Why does *The Return of the Native* have the most examples of the imagery of the printed page? This novel is the one most associated with Hardy's extensive reading and extensive writing in his *Literary Notebook*. [2] As Hardy conducted his extraordinary reading campaign, he not only pondered what he read, but pondered the phenomenon of the act of reading letters, and the strange dependence of preserved thought on these physical marks. Too large a topic to explore here is how Hardy participates in the growing nineteenth century interest in the experience of reading the printed page, forefronted as a self-conscious part of the act of reading and made an analogy for other kinds of human experience.

As we read, then, we wake up like Hardy and see the page as thought for the first time:

> I looked up from my writing
>   And gave a start to see,
> As if rapt in my inditing,
>   The moon's full gaze on me.
>   ('I looked up from my writing', 509)

The syntax has a typically rich Hardy ambiguity. 'As if rapt in my inditing' modifies 'I' looking up, but also seems to modify the moon gazing in on Hardy, as though the moon were enmeshed in the writing. We slide dizzyingly from being immersed in the writing to looking up from it and seeing it from a distance. We see what we read in a new way with that bemused concentration Hardy expresses in 'An August Midnight' (113) when bugs fly into his study:

> --My guest besmear my new-penned line
> Or bang at the lamp and fall supine.

When we re-look at the printed page, we might ask as Hardy does in 'The Walk' (279):

> What difference, then?
> Only that underlying sense
> Of the look of a room on returning thence.

When Jude returns home from his encounter with Arabella (I, chapter 7):

> There lay his book open, just as he had left it, and the capital letters on the title-page regarded him with fixed reproach in the grey starlight, like the unclosed eyes of a dead man:
>   H KAINH ΔIAΘHKH

William Harmon has listed several places in the novels where Hardy, as here, makes his reader look at the 'physicality' of the prose; such moments 'forcibly remind readers that they *are* reading'. [3]

Thus we 'look up' from Hardy's writing and 'give a start' to see the look of the stanza, like 'the look of a room on returning thence'. The look of a room is closely associated with the look of a stanza with its plotted out space on the page. Indeed, the word 'stanza' is derived from an Italian word for 'room'. In his copy of Dryden's translation of Virgil's *Georgics* (Virgil, *Works*, London, 1819, Yale collection), Hardy underlined the following lines (II, lines 59-60):

Not that my song in such a scanty space
So large a subject fully can embrace--

In the margin Hardy noted: '"sonnet's scanty plot of ground", Wordsworth' , a reference to 'Nuns Fret Not at Their Convent's Narrow Room'. We open the page and the sonnet stares up at us, preserved in its squarish form, its evenly hewn 'lines', even its pentameter rhythm defined by the space of the line. Hardy would also sense the cemeterial pun in Wordsworth's 'plot of ground'. The visuality of the stanza has always been implicit in the lyric tradition. But Hardy is important in the history of poetry for developing a consciousness of the visuality of the stanza and connecting it with the tradition of inscriptions and epitaphs.

The printed page, after all, is only a physical object, a design on a field, and itself subject to decay (as our libraries are discovering) like those seemingly more durable inscriptions which wind and rain efface at the end of 'During Wind and Rain': 'Down their carved names the rain-drop ploughs'. (The same force that etches the names eventually effaces them.) In terms of relative fragility, the page is more vulnerable, for example, than the parchment. Thus the barrows left by the Celtic tribes are celebrated in *The Return of the Native*: 'Those of the dyed barbarians who had chosen the cultivable tracts were, in comparison with those who had left their marks here, as writers on paper beside writers on parchment' (VI, chapter 1). But parchment, paper, and even gravestones decay; and where then are the records? In his edition of Shakespeare, Hardy marked the dying King John's speech: 'I am a scribbled form, drawn with a pen / Upon a parchment, and against this fire / Do I shrink up.' Admittedly, we can reprint our pages and refurbish our tombstones, but at what point do our efforts to preserve finally fail?

There is then an ironic edge in the fact that the preserved printed page was, for Hardy, Horace's 'monumentum', 'more lasting than brass, and more sublime than the regal elevation of pyramids'. It was an eternal, or at least sempiternal, inscription. In his copy of Horace's *Works,* translated by T. Buckley (London, 1859, Colby College collection), Hardy read the translation of Horace's ode, 'Exegi monumentum aere perennius', and underlined Buckley's translation: 'I shall not wholly die'. In the margin Hardy wrote the Latin: 'non omnis moriar'. He may have been struck by the oddity, that a piece of the narrator will live in the monument like a saint's relic embalmed. To write is to construct an inscribed object like a monument. In his copy of the *Faerie Queene* (London, 1865, Dorset County Museum collection), Hardy put a marginal line next to Spenser's description of the old historian in the house of Temperance (II. ix, stanzas 56-7):

This man of infinite remembrance was,
And things foregone through many ages held,
Which he recorded still, as they did pas,
Ne suffred them to perish through long eld,
As all things else, the which this world doth weld,

But laid them up in his immortall scrine,
Where they for ever incorrupted dweld.

A 'scrine' is an obsolete word (to be replaced by 'shrine'), a saint's reliquary, a box for holding relics, and this box is compared to the mind of the historian and to the paper he inscribes. In this historian's library is the 'Antiquitie of Faerie lond', a chronicle of 'Briton kings' up to Gloriana, the Faerie Queene, therefore another version of the *Faerie Queene* and analogous to Spenser's own book. The historian's page and the literary work are like an obsolete scrine full of preserved memory.

The printed page was early associated in Hardy's mind with monument and graveyard inscriptions, with funeral epitaphs and carved epigraphs. Tombstones for Hardy are 'text-writ stones' ('The Fading Rose', 737). One of the poems most influencing him was Gray's 'Elegy Written in a Country Churchyard', and indeed the phrase 'text-writ stones' was originally 'storied stones' ,evoking Gray's 'storied urn'. The oddity of Gray's title parallels Hardy's fascination with the inscribed poem, the poem penned in and on a place, and surviving wind and rain as a memorial. One motive for Hardy's preference of poetry over novels may have been the way in which the poem differentiates itself as a printed pattern on the page. James Gibson's edition of Hardy's *Complete Poems* will remain a favoured edition for many because it beautifully presents Hardy's stanza shapes uncluttered by line numbers and notes: we see the poem's shape crisply presented on the white page.

Hardy's intricate stanza forms have associations for him with the decoratively arranged inscriptions on tombstones. Hardy's *Life* begins by proudly reproducing in print 'the tablet commemorating [the Elizabethan Thomas Hardy who endowed the Dorchester Grammar School]...being still in St. Peter's Church, Dorchester, though shifted from its original position in the "Hardy chapel"':

TO THE MEMORYE OF
THOMAS HARDY OF MELCOMBE REGIS IN THE
COUNTY OF DORSETT, ESQUIER, WHOE ENDOWED
THIS BORROUGHE WTH A YEARELY REVENEW

And so it continues in squarish fashion and with appropriate fonts, and given a lined border, to announce that the

BURGISSES OF DORCHESTER, IN TESTIMONY
OF THEIR GRATITUDE, AND TO COMMEND TO
POSTERITY AN EXAMPLE SO WORTHY OF IMITA-
TION, HATH ERECTED THIS MONUMENT.
HE DYED THE 15 OF OCTOBER, ANNO DO: 1559.

Clearly Hardy wanted to end like this, having reversed the declining fortunes of the Hardy family. [4]

Hardy owned a copy of the *A Popular and Illustrated Guide to St. Peter's Church, Dorchester* (Dorchester, 1907, Colby Library collection) which presents intricately carved tombstones which from a distance might be mistaken for Hardy stanzas. Hardy, of course, knew these tombstones well, long before he owned the *Guide*. The *Guide* quotes in its chiselled arrangement the inscription of a John Gollop:

> Johannes e xii filiis Tho Gollop
> Strodae Netherburiensis Ar. Quartus
> Vir admodum Christianus Dorchestriae
> Diu Incola et Magistratus laude
> Dignissimus obiit XXV die Augusti Ano
> Aetatis Lxxxvii, Ano Dom 1731

Hardy was early impressed with these epitaphic shapes which were eventually translated into the stanza shapes of his poems. Thus, for example 'The Monument-Maker' (671) begins:

> I chiselled her monument
> To my mind's content,
> Took it to the church by night,
> When her planet was at its height,
> And set it where I had figured the place in the daytime.
> Having niched it there
> I stepped back, cheered, and thought its outlines fair,
> And its marbles rare.

Hardy also owned Walter Howe's edition of *Everybody's Book of Epitaphs; being for the most part what the living think of the dead* (London, 1891, Colby College collection). Howe's anthology is full of English monument inscriptions like the one to Newton:

> Sir Isaac Newton,
> who first demonstrated the laws by which
> the Almighty made and governs the universe,
> was born at Woolsthorpe, in this parish,
> on Christmas day 1642,
> and was buried in Westminster Abbey, 1727.
> Three generations of the Newton's,
> Lord of the Manor of Woolsthorpe, are buried
> near this place.

From a distance this again looks like a Hardy stanza, except that here the indentations and line arrangement are purely for visual, decorative, and emphatic purposes, while in Hardy the indentations also serve metrical purposes, signalling different types of metrical line. However, the epitaphic background of Hardy's poetry reminds us how important a component in his stanzaic construction is the purely visual sense of the stanza. The last extended example of Howe's 'Epitaphs of Celebrated Persons' is the one dated 1836 to the radical shoemaker Sir Thomas Hardy and illustrating that the

> Most *humble* in society
> When guided by *integrity*
> And aided by *perseverance*
> And *judgment*
> Are sure to add to the happiness
> And advance the liberties of mankind.

Some of the more extended inscriptions in Howe, like the ones to Henry VII, Goldsmith, and Marvell look, from a distance, like ode stanzas. Part of the Marvell inscription reads:

> But a Tombstone can neither contain his Character,
> Nor is Marble necessary to transmit it to Posterity;
> 'Tis engraved on the Minds of his Generation,
> And will always be legible in his inimitable
> Writings

Hardy is fascinated by this phenomenon of legibility, the legibility of an inscribed tombstone, the legibility of the printed page, the legibility of a lasting impression on the brain, and the legibility of a form which somehow remains in the consciousness of mankind though all these embodiments decay. The printed page is made up of simple shapes, yet made oddly 'interesting', 'as shapes intrinsically simple become interesting in writing' (see *The Return of the Native* above).

Howe's collection ends with an epitaph on a sexton, perhaps a germ of a Hardy poem. The epitaph reads:

> Near to this stone lies Archer (John)
> Late Sexton (I aver),
> Who without tears, thirty four years
> Did carcases inter.
>
> But Death at last for his works past,
> Unto him thus did say:

'Leave off this trade, be not afraid,
   But forthwith come away..'

Without reply, or asking why,
   The summons he obey'd.
In seventeen hundred and sixty-eight
   Resigned his life and spade.

Hardy's 'The Sexton at Longpuddle' (745) reads:

He passes down the churchyard track
   On his way to toll the bell;
And stops, and looks at the graves around,
And notes each finished and greening mound
      Complacently,
   As their shaper he,
   And one who can do it well,
And, with a prosperous sense of his doing,
      Thinks he'll not lack
Plenty such work in the long ensuing
      Futurity.
   For people will always die,
   And he will always be nigh
      To shape their cell.

One great difference about Hardy's version is that he is much more sensitive
to the form of his stanza, its mimetic organisation, its appropriateness to his
unfolding theme. His discussion of what the sexton does parallels, at several
points, what the poet does. Like the sexton, Hardy is the poet shaper, and his
stanza shapes inscribe a monument which will live 'in the long ensuing /
Futurity'.

   In his copy of Howe, Hardy made two markings. Next to an epitaph quoted
from Hatfield Churchyard, Hertford (p. 100), Hardy wrote his own preferred
version:

The world's a town with many a crooked street
And death the market place where all men meet.
If life were merchandise that men could buy
   The rich would always live, the poor would die.

Also, on page 153, Hardy put a marginal line next to a Yorkshire epitaph:

> Here lies my wife, a sad slattern and shrew,
> If I said I regretted her, I should lie too!

The pun has yet another dimension, that the speaker now 'lies' indeed in his grave, a dimension of self-consciousness which Hardy was alert to.

Another book which Hardy owned was the *Select Epigrams from the Greek Anthology* (London, 1911) ed. J. W. Mackail. We are now [5] able to examine at Yale the copy he owned. On the second flap, he signed and dated the book 'November 1917' and copied out in Greek the epitaph on Pan from section VI, epigram 10. He also noted in the margin next to 'A Kill Within the Cup' (I,9): 'To Celia B. Jonson. Eyes -- rosy wreath &c added by B.J.'. When we remember that Hardy's great ambition was to write a poem like 'Drink to me only' and be included in the *Golden Treasury* (*Life*, p. 478), we can see how closely Hardy associated 'epitaphs' with the mainstream lyric tradition.

In Mackail Hardy also drew a marginal line next to the first six lines in Greek of 'Dearer than Day', a Silentiarius epigram (I,21). In translation, the entire epigram reads:

'Farewell', I would say to you; and again I check my voice and rein it back-ward, and again I stay beside you; for I shrink from the terrible separation from you as from the bitter night of Acheron; for the light of you is like the day. Yet that, I think, is voiceless, but you bring me also the murmuring talk of that voice sweeter than the Sirens', whereon all my soul's hopes are hung.

Hardy probably knew the Greek Anthology, as he knew these various grave-stone inscriptions, much earlier than the dates of the editions he owned. If so, this Silentarius epigram is one source of his memorial elegies 'The Voice' and 'After a Journey'.

Hardy also drew a marginal line next to the Greek lines of the Simonides epigram, III, 4. Its translation is:

O passer-by, tell the Lacedaemonians that we lie here obeying their orders.

This is an example of a speaking inscription which, according to Geoffrey Hartman, has had much influence on the topographical poem and on the Wordsworthian lyric supposedly rooted in and speaking out of a specific place. [6] The ultimate Hardy example of this tradition is 'During Wind and Rain', the end of a line beginning with Gray's 'Elegy'. Hardy said: 'It bridges over the years to think that Gray might have seen Wordsworth in his cradle, and Wordsworth might have seen me in mine' (*Life*, p. 417).

In Mackail, Hardy also drew a marginal line next to both the Greek and translation of two lines of III, 16: 'Fare thou well, O land that nurturedst me, and thou that thereafter didst hold me, and thou that at last hast taken me to thy breast'. Hardy surely enjoyed the Hardyesque shock in 'Fare thou well ... thou that at last hast taken me to thy breast'. Here, at the moment of furthest distance, we are brought shockingly close to the earth we have said farewell to. Hardy also underlined individual Greek phrases or lines in III, 9 (in translation, 'but they being dead their glory is alive'); IV, 2 (in translation, '[Homer] the ageless mouth of all the world'); IX,6 (in translation, 'not Lais herself knows Lais now'). This last has some of the shock of many of Hardy's concluding lines. [7]

In Mackail, Hardy also marked the translation for III, 57:

Thou who passest on the path, if haply thou does mark this monument, laugh not, I pray thee, though it is a dog's grave; tears fell for me, and the dust was heaped above me by a master's hands, who likewise engraved these words on my tomb.

This may be a source for a Hardy animal elegy like 'Dead "Wessex" the Dog to the Household'.

Hardy also owned William Stebbing's translation, *Greek and Latin Anthology: Part III: Greek Epigrams and Sappho* (London, 1923, Yale collection). In this copy, Hardy marked five poems, four of which are translations of the Palatine Anthology. He marked 'One told me, Herakleitos, of thy fate' and noted in the margin its imitation by William Johnson Cory. Hardy could have read the Cory poem, which he had also made note of in reading Mackail (IV,30), in his copy of the *Oxford Book of English Verse* (Oxford, 1900). [8] Hardy also marked 'Though ye outshine the Moon' and in the margin noted: 'cf. B. Jonson's "Queen & Huntress".' Also, he marked 'Wine I love not', which Stebbing notes is the source of Jonson's 'Drink to me only'. He also owned *Selections from the Greek Anthology* edited by Rosamund Watson ('Graham Tomson') (London, ca. 1889), in which he marked two poems by 'Antiphilus' (pp. 64-5).

Hardy also listed several phrases from Shakespeare under the heading 'Epitaphs' in his 'Poetical Matter' notebook (Yale collection) in July 1915. These passages are interesting in showing how alert he was to the epitaphic potential of certain speeches. The phrases he lists are from the following passages (I have italicised the phrases he wrote into his notebook):

Was't not to this end / That thou began'st to twist *so fine a story?*
  (*Much Ado About Nothing*, I.i, line 313)

But *here must end the story* of my life.
  (*The Comedy of Errors*, I.i, line 138)

There's rosemary, that's *for remembrance.*
  (*Hamlet*, IV,v, line 175)

The record of what injuries you did us,
Though written in our flesh, *we shall remember*
As things done but by chance.
  (*Antony and Cleopatra*, V.ii, line 118)

Julius Ceasar, *whose remembrance yet / Lives in men's eyes.*
  (*Cymbeline*, III.i, lines 2-3)

O my dear lord, / I crave no other, nor *no better man.*
  (*Measure for Measure*, V.i, line 431)

I know *he doth deserve / As much as may be yielded to a man.*
  (*Much Ado About Nothing*, III,i, lines 47-48)

Also in his edition of Shakespeare, Hardy was struck in *Henry V* by the king's boast that he will conquer France,

Or lay these bones in an unworthy urn,
Tombless, with no remembrance over them:
Either our history shall with full mouth
Speak freely of our acts, or else our grave,
Like Turkish mute, shall have a tongueless mouth,
Not worshipp'd with a waxen epitaph.
  (*Henry V*, I.ii, lines 228-233)

Hardy marked the line beginning 'Tombless' and after it wrote 'Cf. Sappho'. He also underlined the last line quoted here, and next to it wrote: 'i.e. Not be honoured even so much as with a waxen epitaph'.

Also in Hardy's copy of Marvell's *Poetical Works* (London, ca. 1880, Yale collection), there is pasted a clipping of a poem supposedly 'Attributed to Marvell' and entitled 'An Epitaph'. The poem begins:

He whom Heaven did call away
Out of this hermitage of day
Has left some reliques in this Urn
As a pledge of his return.

The various examples listed above indicate the crisscrossing meanings of the words, *epigraph*, *epigram*, *epitaph*, the first two only gradually disassociated from their earlier meanings of inscriptions 'written upon' tombs and monuments and walls. Hardy's collected poems make us re-explore these ancient connections between pithy quotations used as mottos ('epigraphs'), short witty poems or sayings ('epigrams'), and epitaphs. In his copy of the *Poetical Works* of Lord Houghton (Richard Monckton Milnes) (London, 1876, Dorset County Museum collection), Hardy put a line next to all the stanzas (except the first two) of 'A Monument for Scutari, After the Crimean War, September, 1855'. Some of the lines describe the kind of aesthetic principle Hardy applies to many of his poems:

> Masters of form! -- if such be now --
>   On sense and powers of Art intent,
> To match this mount of sorrow's brow
>   Devise your seemliest monument.

Houghton's poem is also important because it is one of the inspirations for Hardy's 'Drummer Hodge' (60) and 'The Souls of the Slain' (62):

> Calmly our warriors moulder there,
>   Uncoffined, in the sandy soil....
> No verdure on those graves is seen,
>   No shade obstructs the garish day.

These lost soldiers are 'wept, alas!, too far away':

> Are wept in homes their smiles shall bless
>   No more, beyond the welte'ring deep,
> In cottages now fatherless
>   On English mead or Highland steep,
> In palaces by common grief
>   Made level with the meanest room.

For Hardy, such a poem not only memorialises the dead, it also memorialises itself, a seemly monument which itself is a fading remembrance.

Engraved inscriptions on a tombstone thus not only record impressions, but are like impressions, impressions of the mind, temporarily im-pressed, imprinted. Our very sense of our identity depends on these evanescing mental inscriptions. In 'San Sebastian' (21) the speaker says that 'no deep impression dies', and such impressions are associated elsewhere with both mental and printed inscriptions. When Jude himself is about to plunge into the last anonymity, Arabella momentarily holds his image: 'the imprint on her mind's eye of a pale, statuesque countenance...sobered her a little' (VI, chapter 11). Yet these mental inscriptions are curiously vulnerable. Love and memory die in unconsciousness when 'nought bespeaks you here, or bears, / As I, your imprint through and through' (In a Cathedral City', 171). When Jude arrives at Oxford, he is 'like all new comers to a spot on which the past is deeply graven' (*Jude the Obscure*, II, chapter 2). In his ten volume edition of Shakespeare (London, 1856, Dorset County Museum collection), Hardy marked in *Titus Andronicus* (II, iv, lines 39-40) the second of two lines describing Philomela:

> Fair Philomela, she but lost her tongue,
> And in a tedious sampler sew'd her mind

Shakespeare plays nicely on the physical and mental meanings of Philomela's silent design.

One of the most interesting analogies between inscriptions and ideas is that of Locke in his *Essay Concerning Human Understanding* (Book 2 'Of Ideas', chapter 10 'Of Retention', #5):

> the ideas, as well as children, of our youth often die before us; and our minds represent to us those tombs to which we are approaching; where though the brass and marble remain, yet the inscriptions are effaced by time, and the imagery molders away.

Our minds end like the bare shapes of tombstones which have lost their identifying inscriptions.

Hardy's various uses of a word like 'print' evoke its obscured etymology, originally that of an impression made by a seal, in wax or on a coin; then a figurative usage (now rare) meaning an image stamped in the mind, a 'mental impression' (for example, 'that print...in his conscience', 1583); then any sort of image (the 'prent of his visage', 1513); then a physical imprinting like a foot-print; and then eventually the print we associate with typography. Another obsolete usage along the way would be dear to Derrideans: 'a vestige, trace, indication', as in a 1715 example: 'Scarce any prints of what he had been remained'. It should be clear by now that Hardy's sense of the evanescence of print is integral to his sense of the permanence of print. We have seen Hardy evoked the 'prent of his visage' etymology in describing faces as printed inscriptions. Hardy plays on the physical imprint meaning of print in 'A Sign-Seeker' where he wishes that a deceased lover would 'leave some print to prove her spirit-kisses real' (30). In 'The Two Houses' (549), the old house reassures the new house that it too one day will be filled with ghosts: 'Such shades will ... print on thee their presences as on me'.

If print is etymologically associated with physical imprintation, Hardy connects print specifically with evanescing patterns in nature: 'The twigs of the birch imprint the December sky / Like branching veins upon a thin old hand' ('The Prospect', 735); 'The rain imprinted the step's wet shine / With target-circles' ('On the Doorstep', 478). Or, these natural pages contrast with changing human life: 'the rain ... prints its circles as heretofore'. Or, the print imposed from the outside world seems to enclose human life in an ominous pattern: 'The print of the panes upon them enfeebles ... Until they are left in darkness ... As likewise are left their chill and chiselled neighbours around' ('In Sherborne Abbey', 726) We live in a world of decaying imprints which enclose us, and in whose decay we decay.

Reading poetry, Hardy teaches us, is therefore a little like reading old gravestones, and carries with it some of the puzzlement of such reading: trying to make out an effaced inscription, an old language, with its hidden depths and offering fading though briefly definitive revelations. Something printed is similarly fragile, impersonal, mechanical, eventually anonymous and hardly decipherable, like inscriptions in a neglected cemetery.

Hardy was particularly interested in epitaphs which comment on their own anonymity. In Stebbing, Hardy marked with an X 'It is not my fault', with its funny combination of the epitaph theme and anonymity theme, a weird inversion of Gray. It begins:

It is not my fault you find nought worth reading on this stone;
First to last, nothing happened worth lamenting in my life.

We might call this the self-cancelling epitaph. In Mackail, Hardy drew a marginal line next to the Greek and the translation of the anonymous epigram, III, 65:
I Dionysius of Tarsus lie here at sixty, having never married; and I would that my father had not.

This is a source of Hardy's 'Epitaph on a Pessimist' (779) which also adds an allusion, perhaps, to Stoke Poges, the supposed setting of Gray's 'Elegy':

I'm Smith of Stoke, aged sixty-odd,
I've lived without a dame
From youth-time on; and would to God
My dad had done the same.

Hardy also marked in Stebbing 'Dionysius of Tarsus', another translation source of his own 'Epitaph on a Pessimist', and noted in the margin that it was from

the 'Palatine Anthology'. In answering in 1926 a letter citing the Loeb translation of this poem, Hardy's secretary wrote his reply:

> in the Greek Anthology the epitaph is a mournful one on an unhappy man.
> (A neater translation than that you cite is given in Mackail's Select Epi-
> grams, & a rhymed one in Stebbing's Greek Epigrams.) In the French rende-
> ring (author forgotten) it is changed to humorous, as also in Mr. Hardy's,
> and the French version was alluded to on that account. [9]

Hardy gave the poem at first the subtitle 'From the French', and later 'From
the French and Greek'.

In *Hardy's Metres*, I have argued that a formative influence for Hardy was the
Sapphic fragment, especially as translated by Swinburne ('Thee, too, the years
shall cover'), which translation Hardy called 'the finest *drama* of Death and
Oblivion, so to speak, in our tongue' (*Life*, 305). The shock of Swinburne's
translation is that the reader of the inscription, and the life inscribed, will go
under the soil. Our argument here is that Hardy sees the epitaphic lyric as a
'drama of ... Oblivion', dramatizing its own vulnerability to time. To Hardy's
many references to this Sapphic fragment may be added what seems in fact the
earliest record of the moment when the fragment began to influence him. In
his copy of Aurelius *Thoughts* (trans. George Long), given him by Horace Moule
in 1865, Hardy marked VI, 59 which ends: 'How soon will time cover all things,
and how many it has covered already' (Hardy's underlining). Then at the
bottom of the page, Hardy wrote: 'Thee, too the years shall cover', which he
read in 1866 in 'Anactoria' in Swinburne's *Poems and Ballads*. In the middle
1860s he wrote what may be his first poem from this period, 'Epitaph by
Labourers', the first of many Hardy poems with 'Epitaph' in the title. [10]

Hardy's most famous example of the self-cancelling epitaph is Henchard's
final epitaph in *The Mayor of Casterbridge* (chapter 45). It is written on 'a
crumpled scrap of paper. On it there was pencilled as follows':

Michael Henchard's Will
That Elizabeth-Jane Farfrae be not told of my death, or made to grieve on account of me.
    & that I be not bury'd in consecrated ground.
    & that no sexton be asked to toll the bell.
    & that nobody is wished to see my dead body.
    & that no murners walk behind me at my funeral.
    & that no flours be planted on my grave.
    & that no man remember me.
To this I put my name.
Michael Henchard

Henchard's epitaph looms forth at the end of the novel with a contrarious life,
ironically insistent in its insistence that it not be noticed. While it proclaims its

self-destruction, it is put in the form of a tombstone inscription, demanding to be read. It paradoxically insists on its own preservation and extinction, and in this is not unlike any tombstone inscription which also eventually becomes anonymous. Hardy may have been influenced by Pope's irony in his translation of Horace:

> Thus let me live, unseen, unknown,
>   Thus unlamented let me die,
> Steal from the world, and not a stone
>   Tell where I lie.
> 'Ode on Solitude'

Pope's language is too severe for Horace's gentle moral, and the result is a pun on 'lie', like that which Hardy sensed in the Yorkshire epitaph (see Howe, above) ending 'If I said I regretted her, I should lie too!' What is supposedly a celebration ('Happy the man' etc.) turns here into a scary vision of lost traces, and so recoils back on the Horatian moral. Similarly, the Hardy poem inscribes its own disappearance.

In his copy of Mackail's *Select Epigrams*, Hardy underlined another Greek line which I have not yet mentioned: VII, 9, in translation, 'O my heart, leave the rest alone'. Clearly this is a source of the last poem of Hardy's collected poems, 'He Resolves to Say no More' (919). We can now see that this poem stands as Hardy's final epitaph and ironically alludes to its own mortality hidden behind its stately shape:

> O my soul, keep the rest unknown!
> It is too like a sound of moan
>   When the charnel-eyed
>   Pale Horse has nighed:
> Yea, none shall gather what I hide!

What is Hardy hiding? We are looking at the answer.

NOTES

1 Hardy, *Complete Poems*, variorum edn., ed. James Gibson (London, 1979), nos. 18, 30, 89, 127, 400. References to Hardy's poems are to this edition.

2 See my 'The Second Hardy', *Sewanee Review*, 96 (Spring, 1988), 250-58. Confirming my sense about *The Return of the Native* is Jonathan Wike's 'The World as Text in Hardy's Fiction', *Nineteenth-Century Literature*, 47 (1993), 455-71, a rich article which I came upon after submitting this essay. Wike cites many other Hardy images of print.

3 Harmon, 'Only a Man: Notes on Thomas Hardy', *Parnassus*, 14 (1988), 309.

4 Thomas Hardy, *The Life and Work of Thomas Hardy*, ed. Michael Millgate (Athens, Georgia, 1985), p. 10.

5 The vast Purdy collection of Hardy materials can now be seen at the Beinecke library at Yale. The details in this essay may be considered additions to my discussion in chapter 5 of *Hardy's Metres and Victorian Prosody* (Oxford, 1988).

6 *Hardy's Metres*, p. 177; on topographical poetry and Hardy, see pp. 111-14, 149-60; also my *Hardy's Poetry 1860-1928*, second edn. (London, 1989), epilogue; 'Hardy and Drayton: A Contribution to Pastoral and Georgic Traditions', in *The Literature of Place*, ed. Norman Page and Peter Preston (London, 1993); 'Hardy and Wordsworth', *Victorian Poetry*, 24 (Winter, 1986), 441-454.

7 In Mackail Hardy drew a marginal line next to epigrams, in the Greek, I, 35, 57, IV, 30 (which he marks 'Translated by W. J. Cory' -- see below). He also drew a marginal line next to both the Greek and translations of IV, 32, 40, 47; he drew a line next to the Greek IV, 42 and a check mark next to the translation. He also underlined individual Greek lines: III, 13, line 3; IV, 47, line 4 (all but the first word); XI, 48, line 2 (all but the first word). He underlined and translated the words for 'Eros' and 'Aphrodite' in VIII, 3, and marked the translations for XI, 48 and the second two sentences of 47.

8 *Hardy's Metres*, p. 212.

9 Hardy, *Collected Letters*, ed. Richard Purdy and Michael Millgate (Oxford, 1978-1988), vol. 7, p. 4.

10 See my 'Hardy's Missing Poem and His Copy of Milton', *Thomas Hardy Journal*, 6 (Feb., 1990), 50-60. Hardy's idea of the self-cancelling epitaph is an important development of the tradition studied in Joshua Scodel's *The English Poetic Epitaph: Commemoration and Conflict from Jonson to Wordsworth* (Ithaca, N.Y., 1991).

"A Poet's Idiosyncrasy":
Hardy's Anthologies of His Own Verse

Trevor Johnson

Selected Poems of Thomas Hardy, Golden Treasury Series, Macmillan 1917

Chosen Poems of Thomas Hardy, Golden Treasury Series, Macmillan 1929

The publication in 1861 of Francis Turner Palgrave's anthology *The Golden Treasury of the Best Songs and Lyrical Poems in the English Language* -- to give the book its full, confident title -- was, by any criterion, a literary landmark. This small blue 'pott octavo' volume, in the choice for which Tennyson had so decisive a hand [1], was to give many generations of the English-speaking world their initial, and often their only, overview of British poetry. Thomas Hardy was one of the first generation for whom it performed that enlightening function. His great friend and early mentor Horace Moule gave him a copy before 1862, perhaps for a 21st birthday present, and it almost immediately became his poetic *vade mecum*. He soon began to annotate his own copy, gave one to his sister Mary in 1863 and, as Professor Dennis Taylor says, in so far as metrical exemplars were concerned it served as his 'primary poetic manual' .[2] The proof of the pudding is to be found in the literary quotations and allusions with which he so liberally peppered his early novels. Of the eighty-odd in *Desperate Remedies* twenty are in the *Golden Treasury,* while *A Pair of Blue Eyes*, from over a hundred -- nearly all of them lyrical -- yields twenty-six. To take a particular example, Thomas Campbell's song 'Freedom and Love', quoted in *Under the Greenwood Tree* and in *Far from the Madding Crowd*, turns up again, curiously enough, in *Jude the Obscure.* Probably Hardy knew it by heart.

In 1897 Hardy acquired Palgrave's sequel, *The Golden Treasury Series II,* devoted to the post-Romantics and his own Victorian contemporaries. His response was unenthusiastic; he told Arthur Symons in 1906 that 'There has never been a good [anthology] since the first edition of the *Golden Treasury'.* [3] He never lost his loyalty to the original and, as everyone knows, he confided to his second wife Florence, only weeks before his death, that 'His only ambition, so far as he could remember, was to have some poem, or poems, in a good anthology, like the *Golden Treasury.*' [4] In fact Laurence Binyon had already included three poems by Hardy in the fifth book which he added to Palgrave's four in 1926, and presumably Hardy's permission was requested. John Press's Oxford revision of 1964 realised his ambition more generously with eleven. [5]

Plainly then Hardy had no *prima facie* objection to anthologies. Indeed, he himself made an admirable choice from the verse of his old friend William Barnes for the Oxford University Press in 1908. Accordingly, when in 1915 he had firmly established himself as a poet, with four volumes of lyrics and *The Dynasts* to his credit, including a total of over 350 shorter poems, it was, to Hardy at least, becoming increasingly evident that a selection from his verse would meet a felt need.

The history of the inception, development and publication of what became the *Selected Poems of Thomas Hardy* may be followed in some detail through the *Collected Letters* and in Macmillan's Letter Books. What follows is a brief resume. It seems Hardy aired the idea in 1916 of a 'little volume', initially with Maurice Macmillan, albeit with qualms that publication might have to be deferred until 'after the war'. [6] Nevertheless, he requested and was sent unbound sheets of his four individual volumes, from which he presumably made a 'paste-up' manuscript. Typically, he could not resist the chance to make a few emendations. Perhaps the most interesting occur in 'When I Set Out for Lyonnesse', one of his personal favourites. In *Satires of Circumstance* lines 15-16 ran

> None managed to surmise
> What meant my godlike gloriousness,

for which in *Selected Poems* he substituted the much less orotund and far more effective

> All marked with mute surmise
> My radiance rare and fathomless.

Hardy now wrote formally to Sir Frederick Macmillan asking if he would consider issuing 'in your *Golden Treasury* series at 2/6d a selection of my lyrical and other short poems, including some songs from *The Dynasts*?'. [7] He added that such selections, in his view, tended to 'strengthen sales' of a poet's 'complete works', though there was, in fact, to be no 'collected' edition of his verse until 1919. Sir Frederick at once agreed and Hardy sent up the copy to him on 14 March 1916, with the highly significant comment that 'it has been chosen with a view to general circulation and contains nothing controversial, so far as I see.' [8] Specimen pages arrived on 22 March and were approved by Hardy. [9] He then discussed the choice of a portrait frontispiece (standard for the series) with Macmillans [10], eventually settling on an engraving from a photograph of Hamo Thorneycroft's bronze bust which the sculptor had recently completed. [11] (It was used again for *Chosen Poems* in 1929.)

Selected Poems was accordingly published in an edition of 2,000 copies on 3 October 1916, as the battle of Verdun dragged bloodily on. In our technological wonderland we may still be astounded at the speed with which the whole project was conceived and executed! It contains 18 poems from *Wessex Poems* (1898), 28 from *Poems of the Past and the Present* (1901), 26 from *Time's Laughingstocks* (1909) and 33 from *Satires of Circumstance* (1914), with three songs and three other extracts from *The Dynasts* (1904-8). Of particular interest are the nine further poems from Hardy's -- as yet unpublished -- *Moments of Vision* MS, for which *Selected Poems* is therefore the first edition. He inscribed to his wife Florence Emily on 4 October 'this first copy', containing   corrections and a list of titles ('some at first chosen; afterwards altered') is in the Dorset County Museum, as is his movingly well-worn present from Horace Moule of Palgrave's original.

Perhaps the most immediately notable thing about *Selected Poems* is the total absence of any clue to the compiler's identity, a piece of reticence entirely characteristic of Hardy. More regrettable is the omission of either a Preface or a note on the method of selection and arrangement, for which matters we must therefore rely on inference.

Despite the war, *Selected Poems* was a success, if not a runaway one. A further impression followed in the same month and there were reprints in 1917, 1922, 1924, 1925 and 1927. But the war was probably to blame for the rather scanty reviews, which were, however, generally welcoming. Both the *Saturday Review* (21 October 1916) and the *Times Literary Supplement* (22 November) were commendatory, the latter calling Hardy 'a writer with something to say, and an artist with something to make'. And though *The Bookman* (December 1916) grumbled at the 'absence of lyric spontaneity', *The Living Age* (13 January 1917) said the book proved Hardy to be 'a master in the matter of poetry'. In retrospect one can see *Selected Poems* as something of a watershed in the recognition of Hardy as a poet, and in 1921 the Medici Society issued its text in a fine limited edition of 1,025 copies with a handsome wood-engraved portrait frontispiece by William Nicholson. Fourteen vellum copies were actually signed by Hardy.

By 1927 Hardy had issued a further three volumes of verse: *Moments of Vision* (1917), *Late Lyrics and Earlier* (1922) and *Human Shows* (1925), besides a *Collected Poems* containing his first six volumes in 1923. He thought the time was ripe for a revised selection and cautiously suggested to Sir Frederick Macmillan that 'a slight addition to the selection of my poems in the *Golden Treasury* series might be desirable', adding that there were now 'perhaps a dozen or twenty poems' [i.e. in total] which he would like to add so as to bring the selection 'up to date'. [12] This was, to put it mildly, a pretty sanguine forecast, since his three additional volumes offered a further 468 poems to choose from. Even allowing for the existing scanty representation of *Moments of Vision*, it was hardly to be expected that a mere twenty more poems would do his later work any kind of justice. But, fortunately or perhaps shrewdly, Sir Frederick did not tie Hardy down to his tentative 'dozen or twenty' and by 22 February he had promised to 'go through the recent volumes' for suggested additions. He submitted his 'copy', for which he had cannibalised his 'old copy of *Selected Poems*' still unsure whether he had added 'too many extra ones'. [13] Yet only a week later this indomitable eighty-seven year old was insisting 'in case of any oversight' on reading the proofs. [14] And when he received them he promptly suggested that because some 'stupid people' tended to muddle..."Selected" with "Collected" poems' an entirely new title might be a good idea. Of his several suggestions he inclined towards *Chosen Poems,* which Macmillan accepted. [15] In the event this revised choice and the proof-reading for it made up his last sustained literary endeavour, which reminds us -- for he was still writing poems -- of his amazing creative longevity. He died on 10 January 1928. *Chosen Poems* did not appear until August 1929, in exactly the same format as its predecessor. Indeed Macmillan described it as a 'Second Edition of *Selected Poems*'.

Possibly because of an unprecedented spate of obituary tributes and retro-spective surveys, the appearance of the posthumous *Winter Words* in October 1928 and *The Early Life of Thomas Hardy* in November of the same year, no reviews seem to have been thought necessary and this may have been a contributory factor -- although *Chosen Poems* was reprinted in 1931 -- to the otherwise inexplicable decision to replace it in 1940, the centenary of Hardy's birth, by G. M. Young's markedly inferior *Selected Poems of Thomas Hardy.* [16] Until W. E. Williams' far more generous and judicious Penguin of 1960 Young's was the sole available selection and I would contend that this ill-judged withdrawal of Hardy's own choice contributed materially to the long delay in his acknowledgement as a major poet. At all events, *Chosen Poems* is now a scarce book; both printings are much harder to find than the original *Selected Poems.* [17] Times have changed happily. At my last count, there were over a dozen selections of Hardy's verse available!

Hardy's excessive anxiety to avoid expanding *Chosen Poems* unduly is re-flected in the fact that he made some cuts in his 1916 selection, omitting eight poems in all. [18] The hardest to justify are 'One We Knew', 'A Dream or No' and 'Without Ceremony', albeit he probably felt he had given too much weight to the elegiac series 'Poems of 1912-13' from which the last two are taken (there are still eight of these, out of twenty, in *Chosen Poems*). He partially offset the excisions by adding 'Hap', 'The Fiddler' and the long, powerful narrative 'A Trampwoman's Tragedy', restoring its unaccountably omitted first stanza to 'The Going of the Battery', and including 'Albuera' (in *The Dynasts*) from his earlier volumes.

Then, from his post-1916 work, he inserted a further eleven poems from *Moments of Vision* (in addition to those already included from the manuscript), fifteen from *Late Lyrics and Earlier,* two lyrics from his 1923 verse play *The Queen of Cornwall* -- which I incidentally think makes a case for their inclusion in his *Complete Poems* -- and seventeen from *Human Shows.* This makes a total of 161, or a little under a fifth of the 820 poems then available to him, and it is the product of his mature and carefully considered judgement as to which of his poems were -- subject to certain significant qualifications -- his best, or, and this is an important distinction, his most characteristic. There were, as Hardy saw it, two major inhibiting factors which prevented him from ranging as freely as he would have wished through his large and varied *oeuvre*. Bulk is plainly one concern, but a much more crucial area of self-imposed censorship has to do with subject and treatment. Macmillans do not seem to have imposed explicit constraints, but they had little need to do so for by 1916 Palgrave's initial volume had spawned a hugely successful series, all in identical format, which was ultimately to exceed 70 volumes. Some were popular general anthologies like *Lyric Love* or *The Book of Praise* and others straight reprints of such classics as Bacon's *Essays* or Fitzgerald's *Omar Khayyam*. But several single-author selections attained quasi-definitive status: Matthew Arnold's *Byron* and *Wordsworth*, Stopford Brooke's *Shelley*, and Palgrave's *Keats*, *Herrick*, *Tennyson*, and *Shakespeare's Songs and Sonnets*, at least three of which Hardy owned. They must survive in tens of thousands of copies, laid up to languish forever in dusty school stockrooms. Because the page size is only 6x4" and the spacing lavish, their editors had to concentrate on the briefer lyrics and songs, to the virtual exclusion of longer narratives, satires, *vers d'occasion* and so forth. This restriction on length doubtless vexed Hardy somewhat, but we can view it more philosophically. With a few exceptions his longer narratives are not among his best, and 'The Dead Quire' and 'A Trampwoman's Tragedy' fairly represent the better ones.

Far more intractable problems arose when Hardy came to consider choice of subject and mode of treatment. From its outset the series had assumed a readership including the young and 'impressionable', an assumption reinforced by the rapid growth in demand for school texts, which were often silently expurgated. Mrs. Grundy held a watching brief to which the total exclusion of Donne and Blake from Palgrave's original selection, the omission of Marvell's masterpiece 'To His Coy Mistress' and the emasculation of Burns's contribution all testify. The ethos of the series is summed up by Palgrave's note to his selection from Tennyson (1885) where he insists on poetry's 'natural happy-making function' to 'add sunshine to delight', a restatement of his original contention that he had selected poetry which 'gives treasures more golden than gold...leading us in higher and healthier ways than those of the world.' [19]

To the man who said *his* attitude was best summed up in the line 'If way to the Better there be, it exacts a full look at the Worst' from 'In Tenebris II', Palgrave's effulgent sentiments, if not quite anathema, must have been an unwelcome proscription. But he evidently felt that it was incumbent on him to work within the parameters of the series. After all, the view he had expressed in 1912, that poetry should concern itself with 'impressions, not convictions' [20] could, at a pinch, be reconciled with confining his 'impressions' to those which accorded with the general tenor of the *Golden Treasury* series. His apparent willingness to conform, to avoid the 'controversial', is attested in his letter to Sir Frederick Macmillan quoted above. Nevertheless, the bridle chafed him. He told his close friend and collaborator Mrs. Henniker on 4 March 1917 that 'all poems likely to lead to controversy, and those of the franker kind, have been necessarily omitted -- though they are some of the strongest.' [22] When Gosse replied that he did not grasp 'the principle of selection' Hardy merely said he had 'preferred [poems] acceptable to the "General Reader"'.[23] Plainly, he must have excluded a good many admirable poems on the ground that they might offend the pious, the prudish or the simply naive. It must be an unsatisfactory perspective on his verse that avoids the acrid 'Ah, Are You Digging on my Grave?', that hilarious dialogue 'The Ruined Maid', uninhibited probings of the darker face of love and marriage like 'The Christening', 'Julie Jane' and 'One Ralph Blossom Soliloquises', and his numerous 'obstinate questionings' addressed to God, in 'The Impercipient' for example.

It may seem odd that in this respect *Chosen Poems* does not exhibit a major shift in the policy Hardy had pursued in its predecessor. Was he needlessly timorous? Surely, a decade after the Great War, near the end of the Roaring Twenties, Mrs. Grundy must also have laid down her arms? As it happens, the last anthology in the series to appear before Hardy's suggests caution in reaching such a verdict. H.L. Massingham's pioneering *A Treasury of Seventeenth Century Verse* (1919) does, it is true, admit Marvell's 'To His Coy Mistress' and even Donne's 'The Ecstasy', but it totally excludes the full-blown eroticism of Donne's 'Elegies' and the even more explicit ventures of Carew. The coarse and often scabrous epigrams typical of the period find no place and a quite disproportionately large space is devoted to divine as opposed to secular poetry. Hardy's caginess, it seems, was not as misplaced as we might suppose, and it is highly ironic that right at the end of his literary career he felt himself still to be confronting the same obstacles he had encountered at its outset.

There was a further factor at work in 1927 which must be given some weight. Hardy was, after all, eighty-seven. *Selected Poems* had been, within its limits, a carefully structured volume. Hardy had arranged his choices under three heads: I. *Poems Chiefly Lyrical*, II. *Poems Narrative and Reflective*, and III. *War Poems and Lyrics from The Dynasts*. His categories probably derive from those he used in his Barnes anthology: *Lyrical and Elegiac, Descriptive and Meditative* [including narratives] and *Humourous* (Barnes, of course, offers nothing equivalent to Hardy's third section). But Hardy conceded in his introduction [24] that such categories were tenuous: 'a lyric...may be lyrical and not lyrical to the same reader at different times according to his mood and circumstance' [25] -- thereby placing Dorset about forty years ahead of Parisian critical ideology! And his own categories show some signs of his wanting to have his cake and eat it; 'chiefly' is a useful escape-hatch while narration hasn't all that much in common with meditation. Nevertheless, in *Selected Poems* he took a good deal of trouble both to observe his categories and further to dispose his selections within them so as sometimes to reveal affinities and occasionally contrasts, in ways which the piecemeal publication of his eight successive volumes precluded.

However, *Chosen Poems* was at first intended to be a simple recension and one may take it that Hardy's initial proposal to add 'a dozen or twenty poems' envisaged no more than tacking a few on at the end of each section, an easy enough task for both himself and the printer. Evidently, once he had actually embarked on the task, he soon realised that such a perfunctory procedure would do no sort of justice to his later verse, from which he eventually decided to add forty-five poems.

So far, so good, but the prospect he now faced -- quite apart from Macmillans' reaction to such a radical change -- was of re-arranging the entire anthology *ab initio*, a sufficiently daunting task. Yet now simply to place his substantial additions at the end of their respective sections would have been to invite critical grumbles at such a reach-me-down approach. He hit upon a neat compromise. *Part III* presented no problem with only a couple of additions. For *Part I* he substituted 'The Fiddler', a shorter and sharper poem, for 'News for Her Mother'. He deleted 'Without Ceremony' and 'A Dream or No' (which few would rate quite as highly as those of the eight 'Poems of 1912-13' which remain) and shifted 'Where the Picnic Was' to the end of that group. [26] Then, after 'Wives in the Sere', he inserted 27 further poems. But, it is important to note, these were not inserted *en bloc*, in the order of the successive volumes which yielded them, but rearranged within the grouping. He then picked up the order of *Selected Poems* again with the four poems which had there closed the first section; the last two of them -- 'I Look Into My Glass' and 'Exeunt Omnes' -- with manifest appropriateness; concluding, inevitably, with his personal rite of passage, 'Afterwards'.

For *Part II* he followed a similar procedure, deleting four poems [27], marking the transition with 'A Trampwoman's Tragedy', adding sixteen which he again arranged within their grouping, and ending with the same four, all elegiac in tone, which had ended *Part II* in the earlier selection. Although, for anyone taking the trouble to compare the two books carefully, Hardy's manoeuvres are detectable, it is a measure of his determination and discrimination that he should have taken such pains to present what he must have known was his last survey of his poetry exactly as he wanted it to appear.

Significantly, he also took the chance to move into rather more 'controversial' territory here and there. Thus, 'The Fiddler' glances sourly at marriage, 'Hap' is overtly atheistic, and 'A Trampwoman's Tragedy' hinges on sex and murder, while from the later volumes evil is allowed to triumph in 'The Duel', and 'Fragment' presents the provocative idea of a God capable of learning *from* humanity. But he took only a tentative step or two in this direction; for the most part his additions for *Chosen Poems* are unexceptional by *Golden Treasury* criteria.

It remains true therefore that the *lacunae* Hardy lamented in 1916 were not remedied in 1927 to his, or our, satisfaction. The absence of such admirable if 'controversial' later poems as 'Midnight on the Great Western', 'A Night of Questionings' and 'A Drizzling Easter Morning' is certainly regrettable, but we need to bear in mind that there is a markedly lower incidence of both disputative and satirical verse in Hardy's later work. He would have had to dig much more deeply into his pre-1917 volumes to rectify this imbalance fully. His sardonic humour is also virtually unrepresented, this too being a vein he seldom explored in his later years.

129

These caveats notwithstanding, Hardy's preferences among his own poems ought surely to have served as at least a minatory signpost to his critics. Yet many of them, I suspect, rushed to judgement without taking them into account at all. F.R. Leavis, for so long an ambiguous influence where Hardy's standing as a poet was concerned, said in 1932 that '[Hardy] was a naive poet of simple attitudes and outlook [whose] originality was not of the kind that goes with a high degree of critical awareness... His rank as a major poet rests upon a dozen poems.' [28] This thesis was parroted with variations by a long line of critics. At the risk of repeating what I have said elsewhere, I suggest that the critical naif Leavis posits (a patronising notion long since made untenable by Lennart Bjork and Dennis Taylor among others) must by definition have been utterly incapable of identifying his few accidental triumphs from the dross of what Leavis calls 'a vast bulk of verse interesting only by its oddity.'

Great poems do not come about by fluke; nor was Hardy a literary Douanier Rousseau. Not only did he well know what he was about, but his selections are anything but random lucky dips into a bucketfull of banality. Thus of Leavis's elect half-dozen, 'After a Journey', 'The Voice', 'The Self-Unseeing', 'A Broken Appointment', 'Neutral Tones' and 'During Wind and Rain', all, except the last, are in both of Hardy's selections. That might be ascribed to chance, of course, but there is weightier evidence to follow.

It is now thirteen years since I had occasion to analyse the nine general selections from Hardy's verse made in the fifty years since his own *Chosen Poems*, of which only two were compiled before 1960. [29] I have subsequently added three more substantial selections to my analysis (there are several others which are either too small or too specialised to be representative). What emerges can be stated simply enough. Of the forty-five poems chosen for their excellence by seven or more of these twelve successors in his task, Hardy printed every single one except 'During Wind and Rain'. If I had disregarded J.C. Ransom's notoriously eccentric choice and ignored G.M. Young's 1940 replacement of *Chosen Poems* (which has only 86 lyrics and some inexplicable omissions -- 'At Castle Boterel' for example) these figures would be even more impressive. On the other hand there can be no question that twelve compilers of widely varying critical persuasion working across a span of some sixty years merely followed Hardy's lead. For only two of his preferences are in all twelve (they are in fact 'The Oxen' and 'The Darkling Thrush') and only two more in eleven ('I Look Into My Glass' and 'The Convergence of the Twain'). So much for Leavis's half dozen!

Hardy's successors had *Winter Words* to forage in as well, of course, and some of them also the 27 'uncollected poems' which conclude James Gibson's definitive *Complete Poems*. Nor were they subject to the same inhibiting factors as Hardy in so far as his 'franker' poems were concerned. Nevertheless, the fact that of his 161 selections for *Chosen Poems* over a third have been thought worthy of inclusion as examples of his best work by at least half of those who have followed him must surely put beyond cavil the claim that he knew very well which poems were his best; that he is not the 'imperfectly educated',

critically ingenuous, 'homespun' versifier he was so long thought to be. Rather, as he wrote in 'A Singer Asleep' of Swinburne, his were
> Fresh-fluted notes, yet from a minstrel who
> Blew them not naively, but as one who knew
> Full well why thus he blew.

Even of those poems Hardy chose not to transfer from *Selected* to *Chosen Poems* three ('One We Knew', 'Without Ceremony' and 'A Dream or No') are each in six selections.

As to those poems which are heavily represented in other anthologies but not in Hardy's, it should now be possible to conjecture why he omitted them. For *Chosen Poems* he had already reduced the representation of 'Poems of 1912-13' by two. By the same token he must, however reluctantly, have left out 'Rain on the Grave' (in eight other anthologies), 'The Haunter' and 'The Walk' (both in seven) and the closely connected 'Under the Waterfall' (in six) with others from the series that appear in several selections. He did include several associated poems. [30] The most obvious omissions on the score of their 'controversial' potential are 'The Impercipient' and 'In Church' (both in seven), closely followed by 'Ah, Are You Digging on My Grave', 'Channel Firing', 'In the Cemetery', 'In Tenebris I', 'The Ruined Maid' and 'Voices from Things Growing in a Churchyard' (all in six). No doubt the absence of these and similar poems in what he thought of as his 'Swiftian' vein generated his complaints to Gosse about having to omit 'some of his strongest [poems]' in 1917. *Winter Words*, in 'Lying Awake' and 'Throwing a Tree' (both in six), has two popular poems not available to Hardy in 1926 and he may have thought the subsequently much-praised 'Last Words to a Dumb Friend' (in eight) a trifle too lengthy. I think that 'The Interloper' (in six), with its hint of his wife's mental instability, was probably rejected as too nakedly personal for the *Golden Treasury* audience and that seems to be the only plausible ground for the otherwise unaccountable decision to omit 'During Wind and Rain' (which only G.M. Young -- another of the vagaries that vitiate his selection -- fails to include). These concessions made, there are by my count only four more poems which appear in six or more selections but *not* in *Chosen Poems*.

With the qualifications and exceptions just discussed it can safely be said that a very high proportion indeed of what a consensus of critics and compilers would regard as Hardy's outstanding achievements in the lyric were similarly valued by their author when making his final choice. These, with his half a dozen songs and extracts from *The Dynasts* would account for about sixty of his preferences. But what of the hundred or so others? If those old-fashioned enough to suppose that one poem may actually be better than another complain that some of Hardy's residual selections are inferior, Hardy has two answers for them. The first occurs in a letter to the writer Edward Thomas, whose poems, after his death in the Great War, Hardy was to read and admire. Thomas, who was also working on an anthology in 1915, wrote to ask Hardy's consent to include some of his poems in it. [31] Hardy's reply is of particular interest since he stresses that an anthology should, *inter alia*, illustrate what he calls the characteristic 'idiosyncrasy' of the authors represented in it. By way of exemplification he cites his own 'As I Set Out For Lyonnesse', 'The Ballad Singer' and 'To Meet or Otherwise', all of which he was to include in *Selected Poems*. I think it may be quite confidently inferred from these revealing comments that another of Hardy's objectives in his selection was to proffer examples of his work which display qualities intrinsic to their author; poems which are, one might say, quintessentially 'Hardeian' in what Gerard Manley Hopkins termed their 'thisness'.

It was, of course, Philip Larkin who said of Hardy that 'in almost every poem ... there is a little spinal cord of thought, and each has a little tune of its own ... something you can say of very few poets.'[32] Now as it happens Larkin told Vernon Scannell in the same interview that, when he was 'about twenty-five' and living in digs, he used to be awakened by the sun in the early morning. He went on to say 'It happened I had Hardy's own selection of his poems, and [I] was immediately struck by their tunefulness and their feeling'. It was to this encounter that he attributed his release from what he felt was the much less beneficent influence of Yeats. In his *Oxford Book of Twentieth Century Verse* he gave pride of place to Hardy. It is significant that of the 27 poems he includes four are from *Winter Words*, another four plainly 'controversial' in Hardy's sense, and one from the '1912-13' area, so that, besides 'During Wind and Rain' Larkin hit on only five poems which *might* have been in *Chosen Poems*, as against the eleven from it which he included, and must himself have first read in its pages some twenty-five years earlier.

Of those poems Hardy favoured but which were largely neglected by subsequent anthologists of his verse a quite substantial list could be made. I would begin it with 'Thoughts of Phena', 'The House of Hospitalities', 'Shut Out that Moon', 'Regret Not Me', 'In Front of the Landscape', 'A Commonplace Day', 'A Night in November' and 'The Souls of the Slain' and would add perhaps twenty more. It is only fair, however, to say that several of these have figured more prominently in recent selections.

There remain sixty or so lyrics, besides Hardy's 'War Poems' group, (none of which, curiously enough, Larkin chose), and the presence of a few of these may seem hard to account for. 'Timing Her' for example contains a memorable example of the 'art of sinking in verse' with

> Near is she now, O
> Now, and now, O
> Milk the rich cow, O,
> Forward the tea.

It certainly reminds me of Tennyson's irreverent remark that he thought Shelley's poetry 'All a matter of O!' (though here 'ow' might be nearer the mark). And the opening query of   'Reminiscences of a Dancing Man' --

'Who now remembers Almack's balls?' -- intrigues the reader in a manner perhaps not quite what was intended. There are however further reasons why Hardy thought fit to include poems in various respects less accomplished than the ones earlier considered, the first of which he states himself with admirable precision.

The source is again the only one where he comments directly on the problems facing an anthologist; his introductory remarks to his William Barnes selection. [34] There he contends that

the complete field of the work examined almost always contains a large intermediate tract where the accomplishment is of nearly uniform merit throughout, selection from which must be by a process of sampling rather than gleaning; many a poem, too, of indifferent achievement in its wholeness may contain some line, couplet or stanza of great excellence ... [or] a bad or irrelevant verse may mar the good remainder.

The reader may use his own powers of observation to demonstrate that the second part of Hardy's contention is equally true of his own work; the first may be selectively illustrated by, say, the first verse of 'Let Me Enjoy', the second of 'The Night of the Dance' or the third of 'Great Things', all of which seem to me to reach a markedly higher level than the other stanzas in their respective poems. And certainly, even among what Hardy may have regarded as 'samples' a phrase or a line will light up the page and fix itself in the mind forever; in 'The Curtains Now are Drawn' (Song), for example, with its marvellously atmospheric opening:

The curtains now are drawn,
And the spindrift strikes the glass,
Blown up the jagged pass
By the surly salt sou'-west...

or, indoors by contrast, which comes in the second verse of 'Reminiscences of a Dancing Man':

And the gas-jets winked, and the lustres clinked
And the platform throbbed, as with arms enlinked
    We moved to the minstrelsy.

But mention of contrast brings us to what is evidently a further factor in Hardy's choice; the need to present a conspectual view of his verse in all its exceptional variety. For he knew himself to be protean: and possibly had some qualms about this proclivity. Indeed, 'Rome The Vatican: Sala Delle Muse', one of his selections, was probably included because it offers a veiled defence of his highly eclectic practice. To his 'vision' in the 'Muses Hall' of a 'being divine' who is the 'essence of all the Nine' [muses], he deprecates his 'inconstancy', 'swayed like a river-reed' between 'Form', 'Tune', 'Story, and Dance and Hymn'. She reassures him 'these are but phases of one' [i.e., one art] inasmuch as all are 'projected' from Hardy's 'heart and brain' and thus share an essential unity.[35] One senses here that he is arguing with himself. In 1918 he had noted that the

> glory of poetry lies in its largeness, admitting among its creators men of infinite variety. [36]

There can be little doubt that Hardy regarded his own diversity as a strength, nor that one of his objectives in both his selections was to display not only his 'best' work but also, as he had recommended to Edward Thomas, differing aspects of his 'idiosyncrasy' as a poet. While diction is his most immediately apparent quiddity, this is a critical bone of contention which has been so industriously gnawed already that no purpose would be solved by digging it up again. Nor is anyone now likely to dispute that his range of subject is uncommonly wide. A glance at any section of the index of first lines in *Chosen Poems* will compactly demonstrate his thematic profusion, besides confirming his possession of the quality Walter de la Mare christened 'onset' (which might be glossed as the capacity to hook the reader's imagination on the opening line or two).

If, however, we look at the nine poems which commence with the word 'O' we shall also find that all but two are metrically distinct from the others, and this leads us to the crucial matter of form. For from the outset of his poetic career in 1897 Hardy had chafed at the reviewers' tendency to charge him with neglecting 'form' in favour of 'content'. Lytton Strachey's 'uncelestial music of mutton bones and cleavers' [37] was only one of many similar objurgations. Even in his first volume, *Wessex Poems,* this injustice, as he saw it, still rankled, and he speculated on 'what had passed through the adverse section of the Fleet-Street mind' via a series of syllogisms, one of which runs: '[His verse] must perforce be harsh and clumsy in form, for how can a writer of prose have any inner acquaintance with the music of verse?' This too-evident tetchiness persuaded Florence to delete the passage after his death [38] but I believe he quite deliberately set out to demonstrate his command of form in *Selected Poems* and also to re-emphasise the point in *Chosen Poems* in 1927, by which time he had, as Dennis Taylor has shown, an immense range of forms to choose from. Nevertheless, the table which I append may have some value as a reinforcement of Taylor's arguments in a smaller compass. I have confined myself to verse or stanza form and, selectively, to rhyme scheme. (The Column headed 'Number' indicates the total number of instances in *Chosen Poems.*)

TYPE OF STANZA	EXAMPLES IN CHOSEN POEMS	RHYME-SCHEMES	NUMBER
211 couplet	The Coronation	aa//bb etc	1
311 triplet	In a Cathedral City	aba//bcb	9
	Beeny Cliff	aaa//bbb	
411 quatrain	Wessex Heights	aabb	52
	The Oxen, The Self-Unseeing	abab	
	Neutral Tones	abba	
	The Division	abcb	
511 quintet	The Night of the Dance	abbab	15
	At Castle Boterel	ababb	
611 sestet	To Lizbie Brown	abcbca	20
	When I Set Out for Lyonnesse	abbaab	
711 septet	The Going	ababccb	11
	Men Who March Away	abbbaab	
811 octet	A Broken Appointment	aabcbcaa	29
	A Spot	aabbcddc	
911	The Phantom Horsewoman	abcbcbcaa	5
1011	The Curtains Now Are Drawn	abbcacdeee	4
1411 sonnet	A Church Romance	abbaabba//cddcee	8
	At a Lunar Eclipse	abbaabba//cdecde	
	The Schreckhorn	abbaabba//cdcdee	
Plus 1 unrhymed poem ('Sapphics') and six with irregular stanzas			7
			161 Total

Notes. After the four quatrain patterns which, as the basis both of many hymns in 'common metre' and many ballads and folk-songs were among Hardy's favourites, there are several further variations for each stanza-form in terms of rhyme-scheme. No attempt is made here to show metrical variants, of which Hardy employs every standard variety in *Chosen Poems* besides some of his own devising. 'The Temporary the All' is written in 'English Sapphics' and hence is unique in being unrhymed. Varied stanza lengths are used in: 'Where the Picnic Was', 'I Said to Love', 'The Roman Road', 'Snow in the Suburbs', 'An East-End Curate' and 'Fragment'.

Hardy's reticence about his work and what he thought of it has often been lamented. I have tried to show here that, if we read between the lines of his final selection we may find an *apologia pro poemate mea* which is in some ways more informative and persuasive than his 'Apology' to *Late Lyrics and Earlier* of 1922.

This is, I suppose, the last place to dissuade anyone from embarking on a voyage of discovery into the *Complete Poems*, yet I know its editor would agree that it is a pity the route via *Chosen Poems* is barred to the beginner. For Hardy himself came to regret, as he also said in 1922, 'the juxtaposition [in his *Collected Poems*] of unrelated, even discordant, effusions; poems perhaps years apart in the making, yet facing each other.' None too confidently, he hoped for readers 'whose intuitiveness is proof against all accidents of inconsequence'. [39] In his *Chosen Poems*, despite some hindrances, he was able to provide conditions

135

favourable to the 'right note-catching' he so much desired; to do selectively what in 1922 he had said was now impracticable for his entire *oeuvre*, by 'arranging [his] themes in a graduated kinship of moods'. That was, after all, his principal purpose in *Chosen Poems*; and a careful reading will show how often he attained it.

One may wonder how many of us, at eighty-seven, would have even bothered to try. It is moving to read the penultimate entry in his Notebook for September 18, 1927, 'sent copy for new edition of Selected poems to Macmillan' and to realise that *Chosen Poems* is the record of his last literary endeavour before it could be said of him, as he said of his father

> He has won that storm-tight roof of hers
>   Which Earth grants all her kind. [40]

NOTES

1 '[Tennyson] made the final selection of its contents ... His opinion was the final verdict.' Sir Charles Tennyson, *Alfred Tennyson* (London, 1949), pp. 329-30.

2 Dennis Taylor, *Hardy's Metres and Victorian Poetry* (Oxford, 1988), p. 56 and *passim*.

3 *The Complete Letters of Thomas Hardy*, ed. Richard Purdy and Michael Millgate, 7 volumes (Oxford, 1978-88), III, p. 241.

4 *The Life and Work of Thomas Hardy*, ed. Michael Millgate (London, 1984), p. 478.

5 E. Leeson (ed.) *The New Golden Treasury* (1980) [Macmillan's 'replacement' for Palgrave] has six poems by Hardy.

6 *Letters*, V, 113.

7 *Letters*, V, 132.

8 *Letters*, V, 149.

9 *Letters*, V, 152.

10 *Letters*, V, 161, 169-70.

11 *Letters*, V, 171.

12 *Letters*, VII, 59.

13 *Letters*, VII, 75.

14 *Letters*, VII, 76.

15 *Letters*, VII, 82.

16 *Selected Poems of Thomas Hardy*, with an introduction edited by G.M. Young, was initially available alongside *Chosen Poems* but in 1950 was reset in the *Golden Treasury* format, the stock of *Chosen Poems* presumably being exhausted during the war years. Though Young prints 22 extracts from *The Dynasts* (Hardy printed only seven) there are only 86 other poems as against Hardy's 154. Young does include several 'controversial' pieces but his preferences are very hard to account for. Among his more glaring omissions are 'The Self-Unseeing', 'After a Journey', 'Drummer Hodge', 'He Abjures Love', 'Thoughts of Phena' and 'To an Unborn Pauper Child'.

17 I recently saw a fine copy of the lst edition at 60 pounds sterling.

18 For details see R.L. Purdy *Thomas Hardy: A Bibliographical Study* (Oxford, 1954), pp. 178-88.

19 Palgrave's 'Preface' (1861).

20 Hardy's 'General Preface to the Novels and Poems', *Wessex Edition* Vol. I. 1912: 'the sentiments [are] mere impressions of the moment, and not convictions or arguments'. Cf. also Hardy's 'Apology; to *Late Lyrics and Earlier*, 1922.

21 *Letters*, V, 204.

22 *Letters*, V, 245.

23 *Letters*, V, 255.

24 To *Select Poems of William Barnes*, chosen and edited by Thomas Hardy, (Oxford, 1908).

25 Usefully reprinted in *Thomas Hardy's Personal Writings*, edited by H. Orel (Kansas, 1966).

26 To conform with the changes made in its order after 1914.

27 See Purdy, *Thomas Hardy*, p. 18.

28 F.R. Leavis ,*New Bearings in English Poetry* (London, 1932) pp. 56-62.

29 T. Johnson, '"Pre-Critical Innocence" and the Anthologist's Hardy', in *Victorian Poetry*, [USA] Special Hardy issue, 1979.

30 At least twelve. See *Chosen Poems* pp. 17, 18, 54, 71, 106, 118, 121, 122, 123, 219, 222.

31 Edward Thomas (ed.), *This England: An Anthology From Her Writers* (Oxford, 1915).

32 *Letters*, V, 87.

33 Philip Larkin, 'A Man Who Noticed Things', *The Listener*, 25 July 1968 (an interview with Vernon Scannell).

34 *Select Poems of William Barnes*, p. 24.

35 See *Life*, p. 300, where Hardy returns to the argument, citing 'Rome'.

36 *Life*, p. 414.

37 L. Strachey, *The New Statesman*, 19 December 1914 (review article on Hardy's *Satires of Circumstance*).

38 *Life*, p. 321.

39 Hardy's 'Apology' to *Late Lyrics and Earlier*, 1922; cf. *Life*, p. 448.

40 'She Hears the Storm'.

The Max Gate Library

Michael Millgate

The Max Gate library had its beginnings long before Max Gate itself had been built. Hardy, indeed, once spoke of the collection of books as having been his childhood hobby, although it is hard to think that he was concerned with anything other than sheer accumulation. [1] We do in fact know a certain amount about the little group of books that he had available to him in those early years: several are mentioned in the largely autobiographical *Life* and some of the actual volumes still survive. We also know a good deal about the books that were especially important to him at that moment in his middle twenties when, with what seems almost Jude-like innocence, he set about the task of turning himself into a poet.

Already armed with the Bible and the Book of Common Prayer and the copy of Palgrave's *Golden Treasury* that had been given to him by Horace Moule, Hardy purchased in the mid-1860s such relevant items as Walker's *Rhyming Dictionary*, Nuttall's *Standard Pronouncing Dictionary*, a ten-volume set of Shakespeare, and collections of verse by several of the canonical English poets. Quotations from these and other sources were copied into the 'Studies, Specimens &c.' notebook between 1865 and 1868, thus providing an ample sense of Hardy's reading during those years; on the other hand, it is rarely possible to determine whether or not any individual quotation was taken from a book that Hardy actually owned. [2] For later periods, again, much can be learned of Hardy's reading from the so-called 'Literary Notebooks', now admirably edited by Lennart Björk, [3] but it is clear that most of the entries in the notebooks were taken precisely from books and periodicals that were not on Hardy's own shelves but had been consulted in such places as the British Museum, the Athenaeum Club, and the Dorset County Museum -- or borrowed from Mudie's or some other circulating library.

Apart, indeed, from a few anecdotes in the *Life* about visits to bookshops and occasional references to book purchases in surviving correspondence -- his letters, for example, to the bookseller Walter T. Spencer about the purchase of a Vulgate Bible [4] -- we know remarkably little, either in general or specific terms, about the accumulation of the substantial library which Hardy left behind him at his death. It does, however, seem safe to assume that in Hardy's later years, and especially during the final two decades of unchallenged fame, the continuing expansion of that library was primarily a factor of the rate at which friends, acquaintances, and total strangers pressed copies of their own books upon him -- often with presentation inscriptions of a more or less fulsome character. Publishers, too, must have almost routinely sent copies of new publications in the hope of their attracting the great man's attention. Although Hardy seems rarely to have read such volumes, common courtesy and prudence would have mandated the retention at least of those that had been inscribed or even dedicated to him. On the other hand, Richard Purdy, seeing piles of books on the floor when he visited Max Gate shortly after Hardy's death, was told by Florence Hardy that the many unsolicited volumes received at the house were packed up every so often and sent to a local hospital. [5]

It seems unlikely that we shall ever know on what principle Hardy arranged the books he decided to keep. Those of the most immediate use and interest were presumably shelved in his study, and it seems safe to assume that his move (in 1895 or shortly thereafter) to a newly constructed and considerably larger study was motivated at least in part by the need for more shelf-space than could be installed in the relatively restricted confines of the room -- originally a spare bedroom -- in which he had written *Jude the Obscure*. It would certainly appear -- from the few available photographs -- that the new, and final, study was lined with bookcases throughout, and Florence Hardy once declared that her husband's books made it impossible for them ever to think of leaving Max Gate: 'It would be next to impossible to re-arrange them in another room, or rooms, to his satisfaction.' [6] But since most, and perhaps all, of the study bookcases were subsequently squeezed into the significantly smaller Dorset County Museum reconstruction of the study, and since that reconstruction has never held more than a fraction of the books that Hardy actually owned, a question inevitably arises as to where the other books were kept.

The answer would seem to be, almost everywhere. There were, then as now, fitted shelves, presumably for books, along one wall of the corridor leading from the main staircase to the final study; photographs of the drawing-room taken around the turn of the century show that it contained at least two glass-fronted half-bookcases (i.e., with cupboards below); Bineta Weber (neé Thornton), of Birkin House, visiting Max Gate in 1971, recalled the dining-room as having been 'filled with books' in Hardy's day, with one or more free-standing bookcases in addition to the fitted shelves on either side of the fireplace; [7] and Ellen Titterington, parlour-maid at Max Gate before and after Hardy's death, spoke of the two back attics (Emma Hardy's retreat in her last years) as being 'packed from ceiling to floor with books'. [8]

The study and its contents were carefully preserved by Florence Hardy following her husband's death, and little seems to have been done to it prior to her own death in 1937. The books, however, did not remain entirely undisturbed. Scholars such as William R. Rutland and, especially, Richard Little Purdy were given access to them from time to time, (9) and Florence Hardy, as she had been authorized to do by the terms of her husband's will, gave a few volumes to Hardy's friends, Sir James Barrie, for example, receiving both *The Boy's Own Book* and Shelley's *Queen Mab, and Other Poems*, Dorothy Allhusen *The Oxford Book of Victorian Verse*, Dr. E. W. Mann the copy of J. B. S.

Haldane's *Possible Worlds* that Hardy had been reading during his last illness, Godfrey Elton a handsome edition of W. H. Hudson's *Birds of La Plata*, and E.M. Forster one of the William Barnes volumes used by Hardy in preparing his selected edition of 1907. [10] More important in the long run, however, was the attention the books received from Florence Hardy's fellow literary executor, Sydney Carlyle Cockerell, the Director of the Fitzwilliam Museum and an *habitué* of Max Gate since 1911, when he had first prompted and then organized the distribution of Hardy's manuscripts to selected museums, universities, and public libraries.

This is not the place to treat in detail of Cockerell's relations with Florence Hardy. [11] Suffice it to say that Cockerell, always a somewhat domineering figure, sought in the aftermath of Hardy's death to establish and exercise the utmost of his authority as a literary executor and ensure that the disposal of Hardy's literary remains was handled in an orderly manner -- which is to say, in accordance with his own ideas and priorities. During late January, February, and March of 1928 he made several visits to Max Gate, devoting himself -- sometimes in company with Florence Hardy, sometimes alone -- to the sorting, tidying, and, frequently, the destruction of the notebooks, proofs, newspaper cuttings, and miscellaneous papers that Hardy had left in considerable quantities behind him.

Just as it is difficult not to suspect Cockerell -- and indeed Florence Hardy herself -- of being too quick to burn important documentary materials that might well have been preserved without significantly infringing upon Hardy's privacy, so it is hard not to regret his 'excluding many volumes of ephemeral interest that had accumulated on [Hardy's] shelves' [12] -- books, as he had phrased it in his diary at the time, that ' though not rubbish, did not deserve a place in TH's study'. [13] Cockerell's criteria of ephemerality are likely to have differed sharply from those that a Hardy scholar would invoke today, and it is regrettable that we shall probably never know for certain either the titles of those discarded items or their eventual fates. Since Florence Hardy, in a letter of 8 February 1928, speaks of awaiting Cockerell's 'directions about the books on the study floor', it seems possible that these were the same piles seen by Purdy and that they were disposed of in the fashion then indicated. There is, however, reason to suspect that many of the volumes rejected by Cockerell -- together with yet other volumes, not in the study, that he may not even have looked at -- in fact remained at Max Gate until eventually dispersed in the second of the sales that followed Florence Hardy's death. [14]

But criticism of Cockerell's actions in respect of Hardy's books deserves to be muted. His main, and surely valid, concerns were, first, that the retained volumes should be permanently identified as coming from the Max Gate library and, secondly, that a discrimination should be made and registered between those volumes that Hardy had marked in some way (e.g., by signatures, annotations, underlinings, marginal lines) and those that carried no such traces of his hand, no such evidence of use. With these objectives in view, Cockerell had printed by the Cambridge University Press a simple but elegant book label

141

reading 'FROM THE LIBRARY : OF : THOMAS HARDY, O.M. : MAX GATE' within a two-line rectangular border. [15] As he later explained, the label was 'in two colours: red for books containing Hardy's signature or notes in his handwriting, black for the other selected books'. [16] Florence Hardy wrote to Cockerell on 8 February 1928 to report the safe arrival of 'the book tickets', as she called them, [17] and in March 1928, during one of his visits to Max Gate, he personally pasted red labels into as many signed or annotated volumes 'as [he] could find', leaving the black labels 'to be inserted by Mrs. Hardy or an assistant'. That part of the task, however, as Cockerell went on to complain, was 'not fully carried out' [18], and the failure -- caused partly by Florence Hardy's persistent indecision, partly by the early breakdown of relations between the two literary executors -- was to have unfortunate consequences when the dispersal of the library eventually occurred.

When Florence Hardy died, aged 58, in October 1937 -- a good deal sooner than either she or Hardy can ever have anticipated -- she had still not satisfactorily resolved many of the issues relating to the eventual disposition of her husband's literary remains or, indeed, of Max Gate itself. But while her final instructions as to Max Gate were simply that it was to be sold, she left quite complex directions in respect of the books and manuscripts, specifying in her will that the more important and 'characteristic' of these -- as determined by her executor, Irene Cooper Willis -- should be deposited in the Dorset County Museum, provided the Museum was able and willing to guarantee their permanent exhibition in a 'separate room' described and labelled "The Thomas Hardy Memorial Collection"'. [19] This was the origin of that division of Hardy's library by which one portion was kept together in the reconstructed study in the Dorset County Museum while the remainder was sold at public auction. Given the presence on the Max Gate shelves of so many items that Hardy had not purchased for himself but simply received, passively, as gifts, the arrangement, however regrettable in the eyes of Hardy scholars, was in principle sensible enough. Its practical flaw was that Irene Cooper Willis, though an intelligent woman with impressive literary as well as legal credentials, simply did not know enough about Hardy and his work to make consistently sound judgements as to which books were important and which were not. [20] The result was that a good many Max Gate volumes of some importance were sold by the London auction house of Hodgson & Co. on 26 May 1938, while some relatively insignificant volumes were included among those set aside for the Dorset County Museum. [21]

The portion of the Max Gate library received by the Museum seems, even so, to have been considerably larger and richer than originally envisaged. Florence Hardy's will, while mandating Cooper Willis to select for the Museum 'such articles manuscripts books and letters' as she thought 'desirable or suitable' for purposes of exhibition or reference, gave no indication as to the number of items that might be so selected nor even as to the inclusion or exclusion of books owned by Hardy as distinct from those of which he was himself the author. Evidently it was Cockerell -- looking forward to the future development of the Dorset County Museum as a research centre -- who urged that more of the library should be kept together, not just in order to fill up the study bookcases destined for the Museum but also to prevent the dispersal of books *about* Hardy and books that he had consulted during the writing of *The Dynasts*. On 6 January 1938 Cooper Willis reported to Hodgsons that she had acted on this advice and so 'taken a good chunk out of the study books, which may make some gaps in your lists'. [22]

The reference to 'lists' in the plural is of some interest here, in that Hodgsons had first been asked by the Dorchester auctioneers and valuers, Hy. Duke & Son, acting with the authority of Florence Hardy's executors, to make a 'classified catalogue' of the Max Gate library, including books, manuscripts, and 'literary papers': no 'proper' catalogue had ever been made in the past, but one was now necessary as a first step towards the 'future disposition' of these materials. [23] It does not appear that any comprehensive listing of surviving manuscripts and other documentary materials was in fact made, only the major manuscripts (*Under the Greenwood Tree*, *The Woodlanders*, etc.) apparently being deemed significant for purposes of probate valuation, and if a detailed catalogue was indeed prepared in respect of the books to be offered for auction it must have been sadly truncated and conflated (as we shall see) when the actual catalogue of the Hodgson sale was being drafted and printed.

What certainly was prepared was a typed and admirably detailed (though by no means error-free) listing of all the Max Gate items that had been transferred to the Dorset County Museum (technically to the Museum's controlling body, the Dorset Natural History and Archaeological Society) as of February 1939. Hodgsons' only contribution to the list, however, was to value it, very roughly, for insurance purposes; the actual compilation was done by or under the direction of the then Curator of the Museum, Lieut.-Col. Charles D. Drew. [24] Included were *inter alia*, the manuscripts of *Under the Greenwood Tree*, *The Woodlanders*, *Satires of Circumstance*, and *Late Lyrics and Earlier*, a substantial collection of Hardy's own books (many of them inscribed either to Emma or to Florence), and some 475 volumes written by authors other than Hardy himself. This material, supplemented by pictures, furniture, and what might crudely be called memorabilia, constituted the basis, and almost the entirety -- apart from the manuscript of *The Mayor of Casterbridge* and some other items already in the Museum's possession -- of the Thomas Hardy Memorial Collection that came into public being when the reconstructed study was formally opened on 10 May of that same year. Notebooks, drafts of poems, the typescripts of the *Life*, and other significant papers remained, however, in the possession of Eva Dugdale, Florence Hardy's sister, and of Irene Cooper Willis (in her continuing capacity as executor of Florence Hardy's estate), and the Dorset County Museum's records show that many of these were not delivered into its custody until the 1950s and 1960s. A few, indeed, arrived only after Cooper Willis's death in 1970.

Other items have been generously donated to the Museum over the years by those who knew Hardy, or by their families, but while such gifts are always to be welcomed they do sometimes raise delicate questions of categorization and provenance. In particular, a distinction has to be drawn between books now in the Dorset County Museum that once formed part of the Max Gate library proper and those that may indeed have some Hardy or Hardy family association but never sat on the shelves of Max Gate itself; one of the uses of that listing of what the Museum had in early 1939 received from Florence Hardy's estate is that it constitutes for the Museum's portion of the library a reasonably clear and specific basis upon which such discriminations can be made. Unfortunately the list is by no means definitive so far as the Memorial Collection's holdings of Hardy's own books are concerned: because Cooper Willis had allowed a number of the actual Max Gate copies (chiefly first editions of the poetry volumes) to go to the Hodgson sale, their absence had to be made good by the subsequent purchase of copies lacking any such provenance. [25]

Other difficulties were created for later Hardy scholarship by the deficiencies of the Hodgson sale catalogue and by the breakdown of Cockerell's system of Max Gate book labels. In addition to autograph letters and copies of Hardy's own books, [26] the sale held in Hodgson & Co.'s Chancery Lane rooms on 26 May 1938 included, at a necessarily rough calculation, some 2,000 volumes by authors other than Hardy himself -- representing, it must be assumed, the bulk of what might be considered the Max Gate library proper. But in the sale catalogue those 2,000 or so volumes were distributed among a mere 256 lots, most of them very incompletely described. [27] Thus Lot 153, larger than most but not otherwise untypical, reads: 'Henniker (Mrs. A.) Sowing the Sand, 1898, etc., 2 vols.; Benson (A.C.) The House of Menerdue, 1925, and others, *mostly Presentation Copies to Hardy or Mrs. Hardy, some First Editions* 20 vols.' The number of residual Max Gate volumes sold in the course of another sale on 10 June 1938 can only be guessed at: to the 280 items by authors other than Hardy that were actually enumerated (135 of them in a single lot) must be added 29 'parcels' of books, most of them allegedly 'miscellaneous'. [28] Those booksellers (as they mostly were) who actually purchased at the two sales had of course been able to inspect the lots ahead of time and determine precisely what each contained, but to the late-coming Hardy scholar the record can only seem woefully confusing and incomplete.

It was Sydney Cockerell, in his September 1938 letter to *The Times Literary Supplement*, who pointed out that (as in the instance just cited) Hodgsons had made no attempt to separate Hardy's books from those that had belonged to his wife -- and might even have been published since his death. Recalling in the same letter his abortive attempt, ten years earlier, to identify the authentic Max Gate volumes by means of the red and black book labels, Cockerell also complained not only that some of the original labels had been handed out after the sale itself but also that 'certain booksellers, who did not receive such labels, or who received an insufficient number, have since had colourable imitations of these labels printed, with unfortunate results'. Cockerell was presumably alluding in that last phrase to the poor quality of the printing in the non-authentic labels -- as they may perhaps be called, 'faked' seeming in the circumstances too strong a word -- and it is by its inexactly mitred corners that the one nearest in appearance to the Cambridge University Press label can most readily be distinguished from it. But he seems also to have had in mind the potential for error and even deception created by the uncontrolled proliferation of labels after the library had already been dispersed.

Shortly after the appearance of Cockerell's *TLS* letter one of the Hodgson partners wrote privately to him to report that his firm had received along with the books from Max Gate a box containing several dozen labels, a few of them red, the great majority black. [29] Most had been rendered unusable by damp and resulting adhesion and were simply thrown away, but he had himself inserted some of the black labels in unsigned and unannotated books that struck him as being of particular interest; he had also passed on others, still loose, to four booksellers who had bought lots at the sale -- Walter M. Hill of Chicago, William H. Robinson of Pall Mall, Jacob Schwartz of Ulysses Bookshop, and the Export Book Company -- and to Richard Little Purdy, already well known as a Hardy scholar and himself an active purchaser at the sale through the agency of William H. Robinson. [30] Purdy's labels (retained by him unused and now in the Beinecke Library) are mostly in excellent condition, but the presence of a few that are somewhat stained and soiled suggests that the similarly damaged 'original' labels occasionally encountered in Max Gate books were almost certainly inserted after those books had left Max Gate and quite possibly after they had passed through the Hodgson saleroom. The value of such damaged labels as a *guarantee* of provenance may thus be only marginally greater than that of the 'non-authentic' labels, none of which pre-dated the sale. Hodgson's post-sale distribution of 'authentic' labels in good condition of course complicated the situation still further.

None of this is to suggest that any of the buyers at the Hodgson sales were intent upon deceiving their customers to the extent of passing off as Max Gate books items that in fact had no connection with Hardy at all. But the late insertion of original labels, the large-scale manufacture of imitation labels, and the sheer number of the volumes purchased by the more active bidders were all factors likely to make for confusion, error, and unintentional even if not deliberate misrepresentation, and the combination of these factors with the inadequacies of the Hodgson catalogue itself has certainly created major problems for the project in which I am myself currently engaged, a reconstruction, in catalogue form, of the contents of the Max Gate shelves at the time of Hardy's death. [31] Some of these same problems, of course, also confront anyone concerned to discover whether or not Hardy owned a copy of some particular book, although the possibility of providing at least provisional answers to such relatively simple questions was greatly enhanced by the extensive post-sale cataloguing by booksellers on both sides of the Atlantic.

By the end of 1938 or early in 1939 most of the booksellers active at the Hodgson sales had brought out catalogues of their own, often exclusively or primarily devoted to Hardy, in which they described and priced such of their Max Gate volumes as had not already been privately disposed of -- some dealers having of course bought specific lots on behalf of individual clients, others having distributed advance lists to regular customers or sold items to other dealers: a good many of Bertram Rota's purchases, for example, turn up not in his own catalogues but in a catalogue issued by the San Francisco bookseller David Magee. Because such catalogues were for the most part carefully and responsibly written and described, each volume in some detail, they remain an invaluable -- often a unique -- source of information about Max Gate books whose present whereabouts have not been established. [32]

And an extraordinary number of the volumes auctioned off by Hodgsons do remain untraced, at least to the point of not surfacing during the course of an international mail search I conducted during the autumn of 1992. More than 600 individually addressed letters of enquiry were sent out to university and other institutional libraries in several countries, but while the rate of response was gratifyingly high few libraries were aware of possessing any Max Gate books at all and very few indeed reported holdings of more than a handful of titles. Some respondents, assuring me that 'we do not have any of the Gate collection here', seemed not to have quite registered the nature or purpose of my search. A problem apologetically cited by curators in a number of the more research-oriented libraries was the lack of adequate provenance records, but it is difficult even so to imagine that in such libraries the presence of any significant number of volumes bearing Max Gate bookplates could go completely unnoticed.

The Beinecke Library at Yale holds some 250 Max Gate volumes, most of them formerly in the Richard L. Purdy collection; Frederick B. Adams has some especially important titles; and there are other significant accumulations in the School Library of Eton College, the Colby College Library, and the Harry Ransom Humanities Research Center in Austin, Texas. The British Library has the forty or so items, mostly travel guides, that apparently comprised one of the 'parcels' disposed of at the second Hodgson sale. The Berg Collection of the New York Public Library and the Fales Library of New York University have a dozen or so volumes apiece. Smaller groups can be found in a number of institutional libraries and private collections on both sides of the Atlantic, and individual Max Gate items still appear from time to time in auctioneers' and booksellers' catalogues -- especially those issued by the Philadelphia bookseller David Holmes, who has long taken an informed interest in Hardy and in the Max Gate library. But this remains an unimpressive tally to set alongside the 2,500 or more volumes (exclusive of copies of Hardy's own works) that were included in the two Hodgson sales.

It is a puzzle to know, or even to guess, what can have happened to the remainder. My library survey, though ambitious, was not of course exhaustive, and there could well exist one or more major collections of Max Gate books as yet 'undiscovered', possibly formed early on, while supplies were ample and prices low; if so, and if their original curators are now deceased, their nature and importance have perhaps been lost sight of. Unsold copies still on the shelves of London booksellers may have been destroyed by wartime bombing, and others have perhaps perished in accidents such as the fire suffered many years ago by the William P. Wreden bookshop in California. But must there not repose, scattered through the shelves of various libraries, some hundreds of

Hardy's books, with or without labels, that remain untraceable because catalogued (if at all) only by author and title? Is it not possible, indeed, that some of them, adjudged unimportant or outdated and perhaps bearing no obvious distinguishing marks, have actually been 'de-accessioned' and ignominiously, perhaps irretrievably, disposed of? It would be good to know for sure. [33]

NOTES

1 See Michael Millgate, *Thomas Hardy: A Biography* (Oxford: OUP, 1982), pp. 39-40 and notes.

2 See *Thomas Hardy's 'Studies, Specimens & c.' Notebook*, ed. Pamela Dalziel and Michael Millgate (Oxford: Clarendon Press, 1994), esp. p. xvii.

3 *The Literary Notebooks of Thomas Hardy*, ed. Lennart A. Björk, 2 vols. (London: Macmillan, 1985).

4 *The Collected Letters of Thomas Hardy*, ed. Richard Little Purdy and Michael Millgate, 7 vols. (Oxford: Clarendon Press, 1978-88), III.33, VII.134; the volume itself is now in the Fales Library of New York University.

5 David Holmes, note on conversation with Richard Purdy.

6 Florence Hardy to Paul Lemperly, undated fragment (1917?), Colby College. Text quoted with the permission of the Trustees of Eva Anne Dugdale.

7 Information from Bill and Vera Jesty; on Mrs. Weber, see *Collected Letters*, III.37.

8 Ellen E. Titterington, *Afterthoughts of Max Gate* (St. Peter Port, Guernsey: Toucan Press, 1969), p. 340 (pamphlet paginated as no. 59 in series of 'Monographs on the Life, Times and Works of Thomas Hardy'). I am told by Bill and Vera Jesty that May O'Rourke, Hardy's occasional secretary, spoke of the back attics in similar terms.

9 See William R. Rutland, *Thomas Hardy: A Study of His Writings and Their Background* (Oxford: Basil Blackwell, 1938), p. viii, and Richard Little Purdy, Thomas Hardy: A Bibliographical Study (Oxford: at the Clarendon Press, 1954), p. viii. Edmund Blunden, drawing on Rutland and perhaps other sources as well as on his own observation, also gave a useful brief account of 'the books with which Thomas Hardy lived': Thomas Hardy (London: Macmillan, 1941), p. 182.

10 Barrie's two volumes are now in the Frederick B. Adams collection, Dorothy Allhusen later 'returned' her volume to the Dorset County Museum and Dr. Mann's children have recently done the same with *Possible Worlds*, Elton's book now belongs to Bill and Vera Jesty, and Forster's is in the library of King's College, Cambridge.

11 But see Michael Millgate, *Testamentary Acts: Browning, Tennyson, James, Hardy* (Oxford: Clarendon Press, 1992), pp. 140-68.

12 Letter, 'Hardy's Library', *The Times Literary Supplement*, 17 September 1938, p. 598.

13 Cockerell diary, 5 February 1928, quoted in Millgate, *Testamentary Acts,* p. 159.

14 A few of the discarded books evidently went to Talbothays (Florence Hardy to Cockerell, 8 February 1928, Beinecke), the house in which Hardy's brother and younger sister were still living, and some at least of these may since have found their way to the Dorset County Museum.

15 One of the proof copies Cockerell received from the Press was in the Purdy collection and is now in the Beinecke Library.

16 Cockerell, 'Hardy's Library', p. 598.

17 Beinecke Library.

18 Cockerell, 'Hardy's Library', p. 598.

19 Quotations from photocopy of original will; the text of the will is also available in *Thomas Hardy's Wills and Other Wills of His Family* (St. Peter Port, Guernsey: Toucan Press, 1967), no. 36 in the series of 'Monographs on the Life, Times and Works of Thomas Hardy'.

20 Anyone who encountered Cooper Willis only in her formidable old age will be intrigued by the references to her, with accompanying photograph, in Hugh and Mirabel Cecil's *Clever Hearts: Desmond and Molly MacCarthy: A Biography* (London: Victor Gollancz, 1990), pp. 162-9 and facing p. 160.

21 See Michael Millgate, *Testamentary Acts,* p. 172, and notes.

22 Hodgson Papers (British Library).

23 Letter of 6 November 1937, Hodgson Papers (British Library).

24 Marked copy of list, dated March 1939, and Cooper Willis letter to Hodgson, 8 June 1939, in Hodgson Papers (British Library); additional information from Dorset County Museum records.

25 Lieut.-Col. Drew told Evelyn Hardy in a letter of 3 October 1951 that a few copies not from Max Gate had been added to the Collection 'in order to fill gaps caused by the sale mentioned above' (copy, Dorset County Museum records). See also Millgate, *Testamentary Acts,* p. 172 and notes.

26 Two posthumous editions published by Florence Hardy were present in multiple copies, 33 in all of *An Indiscretion in the Life of an Heiress* and 100 of *The Three Wayfarers*, with a further 110 of the latter (out of a total printing of 250) appearing in the follow-up sale of 10 June.

27 There were 309 lots altogether. The catalogue itself was reprinted by J. Stevens Cox in 1969 as no. 52 of his 'Monographs on the Life, Times and Works of Thomas Hardy'.

28 One further volume, a second copy of the 'Subscribers' Edition of T.E. Lawrence's *Seven Pillars of Wisdom*, was inserted, as lot 46, into another Hodgson sale, on 8 July 1938, while the Hy. Duke and Son auction of the contents of Max Gate, held in Dorchester on 16 February 1938 (ahead of the first Hodgson sale) for some reason included, as lot 184, 'Lloyds Sixpenny Dickens, and sundry books', and, as lot 185, 'Hudson, W.H., *"British Birds,"* and volumes 1, 4, 5 and 6 of Morris' *"British Birds,"* oct., and sundry music': the catalogue was reprinted by J. Stevens Cox in 1970 as no. 66 of his 'Monographs on the Life, Times and Works of Thomas Hardy'.

29 J.Q. Hodgson to Cockerell, 24 September 1938 (Beinecke). Irene Cooper Willis told Cockerell on 6 October 1938 (Victoria and Albert Museum) that Hodgsons must have taken the box of labels without telling her; she added that, in response to a later request from them, she had sent a 'few' black labels but no red ones.

30 Purdy's own records of the sale (Millgate) show that he obtained 207 volumes (33 of them translations of Hardy's works into various languages) for a total cost of £102.1.0, including 10% commission.

31 I take this opportunity to thank the Social Sciences and Humanities Research Council of Canada for its generous assistance to this project, hence to the present paper, and to acknowledge the indispensable advice and co-operation of David Holmes.

32 Among the more important of the catalogues issued in the immediate aftermath of the Hodgson sales were: First Edition Bookshop, no. 33; W. Heffer & Sons, no. 532; Frank Hollings, no. 212; David Magee, no. 23; Maggs Bros., no. 664; Elkin Mathews, no. 77; Bertram Rota, nos. 58 and 61; C.A. Stonehill, no. 141; William P. Wreden, no. 11 (though it seems, in fact, to have been the first catalogue the firm had ever issued); and Export Book Co., no. 287 (in which it is somewhat disturbing, given the firm's access to 'authentic' labels, to find the Max Gate items insufficiently distinguished from those which have no Hardy associations whatsoever).

33 Anyone with relevant information of any sort is warmly invited to write to me at 75 Highland Avenue, Toronto, Canada, M4W 2A4.

President: The Earl of Stockton
Chairman: Dr. James Gibson

The Society welcomes those interested in Hardy's writings, his life and his times. It takes pride in the way in which people come together at its meetings in a harmony which would have delighted Hardy himself. Among its members are many distinguished literary and academic figures, and many others who love and enjoy Hardy's work sufficiently to wish to meet fellow enthusiasts and develop their appreciation of it.

Lectures, guided tours and walks in Hardy's Wessex, Outer Wessex and Lyonnesse, take place throughout the year, and a biennial conference in Dorchester brings together the interested from all over the world. Members receive copies of The Thomas Hardy Journal, published three times a year, and have full access to a large programme of events.

For information and applications for membership, please write to:

The Thomas Hardy Society
P.O. Box 1483
Dorchester, Dorset DT1 1YH
United Kingdom